Acting in Animation

Acting in Animation

A Look at 12 Films

Ed Hooks

HEINEMANN
Portsmouth, NH

Heinemann
A division of Reed Elsevier Inc.
361 Hanover Street
Portsmouth, NH 03801–3912
www.heinemanndrama.com

Offices and agents throughout the world

Library of Congress Cataloging-in-Publication Data
Hooks, Ed.
    Acting in animation : a look at 12 films / Ed Hooks.
      p. cm.
    ISBN 0-325-00705-5 (alk. paper)
    1. Animated films. 2. Nonverbal communication in motion pictures. I. Title.
NC1765.H66 2005
791.4302′8—dc22   2004023993

Editor: Lisa A. Barnett
Production: Sonja S. Chapman
Cover design: Jenny Jensen Greenleaf
Compositor: Reuben Kantor, QEP Design
Manufacturing: Steve Bernier

Printed in the United States of America on acid-free paper
09 08 07 06 05 EB 1 2 3 4 5

For Brad Bird

Contents

Introduction

The 2004 Festival International du Film d'Animation in Annecy, France, presented me with an excellent excuse to interrupt final preparation of this book and head for the airport. Between soaking up sun and screenings, I had the opportunity to share dinner with a well-known character animator. Over mushroom fondue, I told him about the concept for *Acting in Animation: A Look at Twelve Films*. He thought it was a cool idea, especially since a couple of movies he worked on are included in the book. Then we settled into an interesting discussion about what "acting in animation" really means. How much credit or blame can any particular animator give or take for what we see on screen? When we talk about a good performance in animation, whose performance are we referring to? A cursory glance at the end credits of any animated feature today makes clear that no animator works in a vacuum. My fondue friend across the table jokingly suggested that maybe I should consider subtitling my book "Acting for Storyboard Artists" because they are often as responsible as the animators themselves.

He's got a point. I could also subtitle it "Acting for Directors," "Acting for Screenwriters," or "Acting for Producers." I'm sticking with *Acting in Animation: A Look at Twelve Films* but the acting principles on which this book is based will apply across the board. Anybody involved with the storytelling process should find value in them.

My personal theatrical roots are in the legitimate theatre, movies, and television. I had already worked professionally as an actor and acting teacher for twenty-five years when I was invited to teach acting to a group of California animators in 1996. I quickly discovered that stage actors and animators apply acting theory in different ways. The stage actor practices her art "in the present moment," and the animator creates the *illusion* of a present moment. Therefore, when an animator is referred to as "an actor with a pencil," this description is not strictly accurate. An actor is a person who gets up in front of people and dances the dance. An actor aspires to opening on Broadway. An animator has his *character* get up and do the dancing. The stage actor plays for a live audience, and the animator plays for an audience in his head. Big difference. And yet theatrical principles and theory apply the same to the stage actor as to the animator.

Performance Depends on Your Perspective

To the director of a movie, the supervising animator may be an excellent actor because he or she is expert at endowing a character with a dynamic illusion of life.

To the average member of the audience, however, the actor is likely to be the person that does the voice of the animated character. An audience member probably figures Robin Williams or Tom Hanks does all the acting work while nameless animators someplace draw the on-screen pictures to fit whatever Robin and Tom do. The general public doesn't know and doesn't much care whether or not an animator is a good actor. They only care about what they see on screen.

When I think of performance in animation, it includes not only the technical execution or smooth line, but also the construction of the sequence. I look for action, objective, and obstacle. I take into consideration not only the expression of emotion but story development and character analysis as well. Acting choices, regardless of who makes them, are still choices. There is no single "right" way to carry out a performance. In this book, I have a bully pulpit, an opportunity to comment on the work of others. I do so in the full realization that good people may vehemently disagree with my perspective at times. My hope is that these notes will inspire a new generation of animators to think more critically about their art.

How the Movies for This Book Were Selected

Above all, I was looking for clear object lessons that would be useful to new animators or would provide a good review for the experienced animator. I wanted to examine scenes and sequences that work well in addition to those that fail for one reason or another.

I wanted to include different styles of animation, which is why I chose *Grave of the Fireflies* and *Spirited Away* to study alongside *Dumbo*. I seriously considered including Sylvain Chomet's *The Triplets of Belleville* but decided against it at the last moment because that particular movie, as wonderful as it is, doesn't easily provide the kind of object lessons I am chasing here.

Since I am not including the DVDs of the movies with the book, it was essential that my reader be able to easily rent or purchase them. According to my survey, all of the movies analyzed here are broadly available.

Finally, I wanted to include early 2-D feature animation as well as twenty-first-century 3-D animation. That is why I selected *Pinocchio* as well as *Monsters, Inc.*

How to Use This Book

Rent or purchase the DVD of the movie you want to study.

Watch the movie in its entirety. Let your perspective be that of an audience. Sit back and enjoy. Don't think about analysis yet.

If there is a bonus features narration by the filmmakers, screen that.

Read my introductory remarks about the film.

Begin a chapter-by-chapter study. Read my notes for a chapter and then screen the chapter. Read my notes again, and if the object lessons are not yet clear, screen the chapter again.

Acting in Animation: A Look at Twelve Films is a companion to another of my books, *Acting for Animators*. It will stand alone as a text, but you will get much more from my analyses if you have already read and have within easy reach *Acting for Animators*.

I have envisioned myself sitting in a chair next to you as the two of us screen and discuss the movies. Some chapters and film demand more critique than others. That is why you will sometimes see an entry that is only a line or two in length followed by one that runs a page and a half.

Ideally, my reader will screen the movies in the order I have analyzed them. By the time I get to the films in the latter part of the book, I will speak more briefly about certain acting principles, on the presumption that you do not need to see everything repeated in full with each film.

Regarding Movie Production Credits

The listed credits are necessarily incomplete. Producers of early animated feature films were stingy with screen credits, even for some of their more important animators, and producers of modern animated movies tend to overcredit. They want to put on screen the names of the entire legal department, for example, plus the names of every assistant. To be sure, everybody working on a movie is important, and a modern film production employs vast numbers of artists and technicians. Since the scope of this book is restricted to performance, however, I have tried to include listings of those people most likely to have input or influence on story and character. I have left out contributors to visual effects, special effects, and music most of the time.

Some Essential Acting Principles

Acting theory is a very lovely thing once you get the hang of it. It has the form of a well-constructed musical score. Many acting principles can be approached from different angles. In other words, you can say the same thing in different ways. The following seven principles are fundamental to my approach. Read them over, and if you want early amplification, check *Acting for Animators*.

1. A scene is a negotiation. In any negotiation, there must be a way you can win and a way you can lose.
2. Thinking tends to lead to conclusions; emotion tends to lead to action.
3. Play an action until something happens to make you play a different action.
4. Theatrical reality is not the same thing as regular reality. Theatrical reality has form and is compressed in time and space.
5. Empathy is the key to effective performance animation. Humans empathize only with emotion, not with thinking.
6. Constantin Stanislavsky defined acting as "playing an action in pursuit of an objective while overcoming an obstacle." In an acting sense, an obstacle is the same thing as conflict. Conflict does not have to be a negative thing or a fistfight. In life, we generally try to avoid conflict, but in acting, it is our friend.
7. There are only three kinds of conflict (obstacle): (1) conflict with self; (2) conflict with the situation; and (3) conflict with another character.

1. Charlotte's Web

A Hanna-Barbera Production released by Paramount Pictures (1973)

Producers: William Hanna, Joseph Barbera

Directors: Charles A. Nichols, Iwao Takamoto

Story: Earl Hamner Jr. (based on the book by E. B. White)

Key Animators: Hal Ambro, Ed Barge, Lars Galonius, Dick Lundy, Irv Spence

Animators: Ed Aardal, Lee Dyer, Bob Gow, George Kreisl, Don Patterson, Carlo Vinci, O. E. Callahan, Hugh Fraser, Volus Jones, Ed Parks, Ray Patterson, Xenia

Voice Cast: Debbie Reynolds (Charlotte), Henry Gibson (Wilbur), Paul Lynde (Templeton), Pamelyn Ferdin (Fern Arable), Joan Gerber (Mrs. Zuckerman, Mrs. Fussy, Old Lady, Operator), Robert Holt (Homer Zuckerman), Dave Madden (Ram/others), Don Messick Geoffrey (Lamb, Uncle, Bystanders), Dave Madden (Old Ram), Danny Bonaduce (Avery Arable), Agnes Moorehead (The Goose), Martha Scott (Mrs. Arable), John Stephenson (Farmer Arable, Judge, Bandleader, Guard), Herb Vigran (Lurvy), William B. White (Henry Fussy), Charles Nelson Reilly, Rex Allen (Narrator)

Overview

Charlotte's Web, a perennial favorite of six- to nine-year-old children, is proof positive that if you start with a good story that is targeted to the right audience, you'll have a lasting success even if the animation isn't extraordinary.

The original book by E. B.White (1899–1985), on which the movie is based, is ingenious and shamanistic. The farm saga of Wilbur the runt piglet and his lifesaving friendship with Charlotte the grey spider is simultaneously a delightful tale of salvation and a basic primer on the behavior and habits of barnyard animals and insects. The reader/viewer makes friends with the animals while learning, among other things, that spiders suck the blood of insects, that pigs sometimes faint just like humans, and that there is a seasonal cycle to life on the farm. He learns about county fairs and that the fate of most farm pigs is eventually to be turned into bacon. And he learns that all creatures in the world die, some sooner than later.

The animation in *Charlotte's Web,* produced by Hanna and Barbera and directed by Nichols and Takamoto, is the very definition of simplicity, but then six- to nine-year-old kids are forgiving. If you were to remove the celebrity voices and just watch the animation, the screen would often appear lifeless. The only character that has real on-screen personality is Templeton the rat, voiced by the fabulous Paul Lynde. Templeton is mischievous and smart, often reminding me of the Tom and Jerry cartoons, which were coincidentally also created by Hanna and Barbera.

The big challenge for the *Charlotte's Web* production team was to get the audience to empathize with the barnyard animals. In particular, they had to make us care about Wilbur the pig. The way they accomplish this is brilliant and seamless: They introduce the animals first from a human's point of view (POV) and then, in Chapter 3 of the DVD, they abruptly shift the POV

2

to favor the animals. After Chapter 3, instead of seeing animals from a human POV, we see humans from an animal POV. The animators gradually humanized the physical behavior of certain animals. The only thing remaining by the end of Chapter 2 was to hear the animals talk, and that is what is added in Chapter 3. Once they are talking, we are totally immersed in their world.

The way the movie deals with obstacle/conflict is also significant. As we know, there are three kinds of conflict— (1) conflict with self; (2) conflict with situation; and (3) conflict with another character. *Charlotte's Web,* **almost without exception, uses only conflict with situation.** At first this puzzled me, but the more I thought about it the more brilliant I thought it was. The movie is targeted to very young children who, in their own lives, mainly have conflict with the situation. They are too short to reach the cookie jar; Mom won't let them go out in the rain without their boots; they can't eat their dessert before they eat their peas. Children that age do not get into heavyweight considerations of life, which would lead to conflict with self. And the conflict they have with parents isn't really conflict because the parents are their caretakers. The conflict they have with other children is also lightweight as a rule—a bloody nose, maybe, or some lost marbles, but children rarely do true damage to one another. The stakes are pretty low. *Charlotte's Web* is a perennial favorite, even after all these years, because it is the perfect movie for the perfect audience.

Analysis

Chapter 1: "Before Breakfast"

We meet the wholesome and folksy Arable family and get our first glimpse of their lovely, fertile farm. It is springtime and a newborn litter of piglets is happily nursing. All except one, that is—the runt of the litter. He can't find room at mama pig's teat. **Conflict with the situation.** The runt (Wilbur, but we don't know his name yet) tries repeatedly to find a nipple and gets bounced back on his behind.

John Arable decides to destroy the runt piglet, but his daughter, Fern, tearfully springs to the piglet's rescue. There are two acting notes involved here: (1) **Emotion tends to lead to action.** (2) Fern has **conflict with the situation** as well as **conflict with another character** (her father). In order to get the audience to empathize with the piglet, it is necessary to humanize him. The animators begin this process the moment Wilbur is placed into Fern's arms. Note that the pig's behavior is a spot-on copy of a human infant's smiling and cooing behavior.

Wilbur's near execution is an adrenaline moment for Fern. An adrenaline moment is one that the character will remember when she turns eighty-five years old and looks back on her life. It is virtually impossible to tell a compelling story without at least one adrenaline moment. It is probably not one for her father because he is accustomed to slaughtering farm animals, nor would it be one for Wilbur because he is too young to know what is going on.

Later, at the breakfast table, a syrupy pancake lands on Wilbur's head. Note that he licks at the sweet syrup with his mouth the way a human baby would. Also, he smiles a human smile. Pigs don't express emotion with a smile in real life, and they don't have crinkly eyes with pretty eyelashes.

Chapter 2: "Wilbur"

Further personification of Wilbur the pig. Fern, now functioning as Wilbur's surrogate mama, bathes the baby pig, sings to him, plays hide-and-seek with him, and so on. **All of this is pure exposition and humanization, designed to get the viewer to** empathize with Wilbur. **There is zero conflict.** By the time we get to the sequence about Wilbur having to sleep in his own bed alone, outside the house, the viewer has been captured emotionally. **The sequence also contains conflict with the situation.** We can all remember what it was like as a kid to be afraid of the dark. (*Monsters, Inc.* would capitalize on this same childhood memory twenty-three years later.)

Chapter 3: "Loneliness"

At six weeks old, Wilbur is sold to Fern's uncle. **The tearful goodbye between Fern and Wilbur works on multiple levels. We empathize with both of them.** A mother would grieve if her child was snatched from her life, and the child would cry and resist going. Also, Wilbur is, for the first time, in a cage. Like a prisoner, he is trapped and helpless. And so the audience's emotional reaction to this scene is probably the strongest so far in the film.

The story now shifts to another farm and a new location. We soon begin hearing the animals "talk" for the first time as we enter fully into the animal world. In Chapters 1 and 2, we observed the animals from the human perspective. After the transition to the new farm, we view humans from the animals' perspective. Our worldview is turned upside down. It is quite a brilliant storytelling device. It would have been difficult to make the worldview transition without making a physical transition from one location to another.

When Wilbur is trying to find his voice for the first time, the Goose urges him on by chanting, "Try! Try! Try!" This theme runs throughout the movie. **We act to survive.** If Wilbur had tried to speak and then given up the effort, the scene would have failed.

Wilbur breaks the fourth wall, addressing the camera and the viewer. He sings "I can talk!" **Emotion tends to lead to**

action. When he realizes he can talk, he jumps into the air with glee, even bounds to the top of a fence post—something a pig would never, ever do. More humanization. **Play an action until something happens to make you play a different action.** Wilbur sings until he notices that the Ram is annoyed. The song ends immediately after Wilbur's facial reaction to the Ram's angry glare.

Emotion tends to lead to action. After the happy song is over, Wilbur is overcome with sadness. "I miss Fern," he tells the Goose. Then he sags to the ground. The energy goes out of his body, propelled by the emotion of sadness. The animator could have simply left it with the line, "I miss Fern." Following that declaration with the sagging to the ground establishes a bit of conflict with the situation, so the moment is milked for a little more storytelling juice.

We start meeting other animals. Templeton the rat (Paul Lynde) is the most colorful and best-animated character in *Charlotte's Web*. His characterization frequently reminds me of Tom and Jerry cartoons, which Hanna and Barbera also created.

The Ram informs Wilbur that he is destined to be turned into "smoked bacon." **Conflict with the situation.** "I don't want to die!" Wilbur bawls, his tears flying as he beats the ground with his feet. At the end of the sequence, we hear Charlotte's soothing voice for first time, urging Wilbur to get a grip on himself.

Chapter 4: "Charlotte"

This is an adrenaline moment for Wilbur. He will never forget the day he first met Charlotte. In performance Charlotte remains spiderlike for the entire movie. Everything about her is communicated via the Debbie Reynolds voice-over. The dramatic device here is that Charlotte is all-knowing and wise, another surrogate parent figure to Wilbur. She will teach him to accept life for what it is, to realize he can do what he wants to do if he only tries, and to understand that life is temporary. She also educates him and the viewer about the value of spiders in the world. The main purpose of the sequence is to introduce Charlotte and to establish her relationship with Wilbur.

Chapter 5: "Summer Days"

Note that by this point in the film, all of the barn animals have more humanlike eye expression. It's crude, but it's there. This helps establish empathy.

The primary point of this chapter is to establish that Fern has a vivid imagination and can hear the animals talk. Her parents, of course, think she has been spending too much time alone in the barn. She protests, "I'm not alone. My best friends are in the barn." This is clever on the part of the storytellers. Most children have an active imagination and it is not uncommon for them to carry on "conversations" with animals. We can empathize with the emotions involved.

Also, Jeffrey, the runt gosling, likes to hang around with Wilbur instead of his own goose mom. The runt of one litter has a connection to the runt of another.

Chapter 6: "The Miracle"

This chapter contains the title song, "Charlotte's Web," a dreamlike lullaby about what happens at night when the spider is weaving and spinning her web. It's really pretty and has probably put countless children to sleep in front of the television.

At sunup, all the barnyard animals discover that Charlotte has woven into her web the words "Some Pig." **For the humans on the farm, this is an adrenaline moment. They think they're seeing a miracle, and people will always remember the day they saw a miracle.** Wilbur is suddenly a celebrity. Articles are written about him in the newspapers and many visitors come to see the miracle web.

A wasp gets caught in Charlotte's web and wrecks it. Wilbur is afraid that without the words in the web, nobody will believe in the miracle any longer and he will be made into bacon. As the web is destroyed, Wilbur has **conflict with situation.**

Chapter 7: "A Meeting"

Lesson in life: Two heads are better than one. Charlotte calls a meeting of all the animals, asking for help in coming up with a new web message. All the animals have **conflict with situation** as they try to think of a new saying.

Chapter 8: "Good Progress"

Templeton is sent to search for something with writing on it that can be used for inspiration. He finds a piece of a soap flakes box. The words on it are "with new radiant action."

Note that the Templeton animation is stronger than the animation for the other animals. When he is sneaking around in the garbage dump, tumbling down the hill in a soup can, and so on, the animation almost springs to life. What they did with Templeton in this movie makes you long for more of the same with the other animals.

Wilbur performs "radiantly" for the assembled animals, and so Charlotte weaves the word "radiant" into her web.

Fame returns and Homer Zuckerman decides to take Wilbur to the county fair. Big celebration! **This is an adrenaline moment for all the animals and insects.**

The Goat tells Wilbur that if he doesn't win a prize at the fair, he'll be bacon. This of course makes Wilbur nervous once again and increases the amount of conflict with the situation he experiences. He asks Charlotte to accompany him to the fair.

She tells him that all that matters in the contest is character. "You have a lot of character, Wilbur," she assures him.

Then we learn that Charlotte is going to make an egg sac in preparation for her babies. And we get another song, "Mother Earth and Father Time," explaining the life cycle to us one more time.

Chapter 9: "Off to the Fair"

Charlotte and Templeton go with Wilbur to the county fair.

Wilbur plays to the expectations of the group and resists getting into his crate even though he is not opposed to it. The reasoning is that, if he doesn't act like a pig, they'll think something is wrong with him. I think this is a very clever character choice.

Fern, growing up now, meets Henry Fussy at the fair. Shades of Thornton Wilder's famous stage play *Our Town*. Boy meets girl, holding hands. Wilbur feels abandoned, but Charlotte reassures him that it is just life and that Fern is looking at Henry Fussy "through new eyes."

Note that, once the action shifts to the county fair, the animals start to be less like humans and more like animals. Wilbur is grunting like a pig. Other animals have no humanization at all. This will reflect reality to the children who watch the movie. Probably they have been to a county fair or carnival one time or another, and the animals there are real animals. The worldview is shifted a bit away from seeing humans through animal eyes and back to seeing animals through human eyes.

Chapter 10: "Uncle"

Charlotte meets Uncle, the pig in the stall next to Wilbur's at the fair. He is formidable competition, but she thinks she can put Wilbur over the top.

Charlotte is conspicuously slowing down now, coming to the end of her life cycle. This is a form of **conflict with the situation** for her. **One way to increase conflict with the situation is to have the character race against time.** She must ensure that Wilbur wins a prize before her death.

Chapter 11: "The Cool of the Evening"

Templeton finds a piece of paper at the fair, with the word "Humble" written on it. Charlotte figures she can use that in her web.

Templeton gorges himself on leftover goodies at the fair during the night. Again, the animation of Templeton is quite a bit stronger and more . . . mmm . . . animated than that of the other animals. He eats so much, his belly swells to triple its regular size and he seems almost drunk.

Chapter 12: "The Egg Sac"

Wilbur wakes up and discovers that Charlotte has made an egg sac that contains, according to her, five hundred and fourteen eggs. It is her magnum opus, her life's greatest achievement.

Charlotte is increasingly tired. She tells Wilbur she is getting old, feeling her age.

Templeton shows up after the long night of gorging. He's going to have a terrible hangover.

Chapter 13: "The Hour of Triumph"

Fern and the other humans discover that Charlotte has woven into her web, in big glowing letters, the word "HUMBLE." Anticipating victory at the fair, they instead discover that Uncle in the next stall has been awarded first prize already. Everybody is sad and crying, especially Fern, because she thinks Wilbur will now become bacon. **Conflict with situation.**

Just as things are looking terribly bleak, a colorful marching band arrives and Wilbur is awarded a special prize because he has been so good for state tourism.

Chapter 14: "Last Day"

Charlotte dies. This is an adrenaline moment for Wilbur.

Chapter 15: "A Warm Wind"

Wilbur carries Charlotte's egg sac back to the barn in his mouth and watches over it until spring.

Babies are born, making Wilbur happy, but then they all begin to float away to other places where they would make new webs. Wilbur cries and threatens to run away. Then he discovers that there were three runt spider babies that are too small to fly away. They will stay with Wilbur on the farm, and everybody will live happily ever after.

2. Dumbo

A Walt Disney Production (1941)

Producer: Walt Disney

Director: Ben Sharpsteen

Writers: Helen Aberson (Book), Aurie Battaglia, Otto Englander, Joe Grant, Dick Huemer, Bill Peet, Harold Perl (Book), Joe Rinaldi, Webb Smith, George Stallings

Sequence Directors: Samuel Armstrong, Norman Ferguson, Wilfred Jackson, Jack Kinney, Bill Roberts

Animator Directors: Art Babbitt, Ward Kimball, John Lounsbery, Fred Moore, Wolfgang Reitherman, Vladimir (Bill) Tytla

Voice Cast: Herman Bing (Ringmaster), Billy Bletcher (Clown), Edward Brophy (Timothy Q. Mouse), Jim Carmichael (Crow), Hall Johnson Choir (Crows), Cliff Edwards (Jim Crow), Verna Felton (Elephant Matriarch), Noreen Gammill (Elephant), Sterling Holloway (Mr. Stork), Malcolm Hutton (Skinny), Harold Manley (Boy), John McLeish (Narrator), Tony Neil (Boy), Dorothy Scott (Elephant), Sarah Selby (Elephant), Billy Sheets (Joe/Clown), Chuck Stubbs (Boy), Margaret Wright (Casey Jr.)

Overview

Back in 1941, the style of animation contained much more pantomime than it does today. Notice how Timothy Q. Mouse, for instance, continually illustrates the spoken word with generic gesture. There was evidently no consideration at all of such things as Chekhov's Psychological Gesture. Dumbo's tears are also interesting. Vladimir (Bill) Tytla was the animation director for Dumbo, and boy, did he ever capture the illusion of emotion! Elephants are rumored to cry, but my research is that they do not in fact cry. According to *Crying: A Natural and Cultural History of Tears* (Tom Lutz, W. W. Norton, 2001) only humans cry tears of sadness. Reflection of reality or not, animal tears are often used in animation to elicit empathy.

Analysis

Chapter 1: Opening Credits

Chapter 2: "Look Out for Mister Stork"

The storks deliver babies to the circus. At the end of the sequence, we first meet Mrs. Jumbo, whose baby is late in arriving. She stretches her trunk into the night sky, searching in vain for her baby. Note that her gaze and thought processes are quite specific. She focuses on the incoming baby/parachute to her left and follows it hopefully as it descends from the sky. When it floats into another animal's area, her thought process is, "That's not my baby. . . ." Then she returns to searching the sky. Another baby/parachute descends to her right and she hopefully follows that one as it, too, floats into another animal's area. Then she again searches the sky. No more baby/parachutes. Her thought is, "My baby is not coming tonight. . . ." And she sags a bit in disappointment. **A scene is a negotiation. Mrs. Jumbo is playing an action (searching the sky for her baby), in pursuit of an objective (trying to find her baby), while overcoming an obstacle (conflict with the situation). Also: Play an action until something happens to make you play a different action.** She follows each baby/parachute, first with hope and then with disappointment. When she is certain that one of them is not hers she returns to the search. One thought and action at a time.

Chapter 3: "The Circus Moves On"

Mainly a series of connective and expository sequences, establishing that the circus is going to another town.

Chapter 4: "Delivery for Mrs. Jumbo"

Also a series of connective and expository sequences, but these have slightly more conflict (obstacles). **The stork sitting on the cloud has conflict with the situation as he searches for the precise location of Mrs. Jumbo down below.** Once he finds the moving train, he has further conflict with the situation as he searches for the particular car that holds Mrs. Jumbo. Once he finds Mrs. Jumbo, there is slight conflict between the stork and Mrs. Jumbo. She wants to get on with mothering her baby, and the stork wants to go through formalities first, singing Happy Birthday and so on. **This is, by the way, an adrenaline moment for Mrs. Jumbo.** Mrs. Jumbo will always remember the day her baby was born on the moving train. When the stork departs, the level of conflict (between characters) increases as the other elephant matrons make fun of Dumbo's ears. Mrs. Jumbo physically swats them away with her trunk and then sweetly cradles her baby.

Chapter 5: "Setting Up the Big Top"

Expository/connective sequences with very mild conflict as Dumbo learns how to do his part in the circus migration. **He is in conflict with the situation due to his small size, big ears, and unfamiliarity with the process.** At the end of the chapter, he trips on his ears and falls in the mud. Again, conflict with the situation.

Chapter 6: "A Bath for Dumbo"

This is an important series of sequences. It begins by establishing a zero-conflict loving relationship between Dumbo and his mother as she bathes him and plays hide-and-seek. In that sense, this sequence is mainly a connective scene. The audience is lulled into empathic comfort. Then the scene arcs sharply as the human children arrive to taunt Dumbo. **Mrs. Jumbo first has conflict with the situation; then as the redheaded boy physically grabs Dumbo and blows in his ear, conflict with situation changes into conflict with another character.** Mrs. Jumbo turns red-eyed and defends her baby. She turns the red-haired boy over and spanks him. **Emotion tends to lead to action.** The circus ringmaster comes in with his whip, which further escalates the conflict between characters. Mrs. Jumbo is subdued with ropes and is separated from her baby. **This scene is surely an adrenaline moment, too.**

Chapter 7: "Mrs. Jumbo in Solitary Confinement"

The sequences begin by establishing the emotional pain of separation. **Conflict with situation.** Note that Dumbo tries to be even smaller, hunkering into a corner. **That is a status transaction. A character with low self-esteem or sadness will generally**

try to take up less space in the world. Dumbo comforts himself by gently swaying back and forth, the same kind of movement involved when his mother rocks him. This was foreshadowed at the end of Chapter 4. **Emotion tends to lead to action. The emotion is sadness; the action is to comfort himself. Conflict/ obstacle is with the situation.** Then we meet Timothy Q. Mouse. He is immediately established as an ally of Dumbo when he scares the cruel and gossipy matron elephants. When Dumbo moves to join the older elephants, they close ranks, blocking him out. His action remains to comfort himself, but the kind of conflict involved shifts from conflict with the situation and onto conflict with other characters. **He then plays an action until something happens to make him play another action.** When he is blocked from the group, he changes direction and goes off to hide under some hay.

Chapter 8: "Dumbo Meets a New Friend"

Mainly an expository/connective scene in which the relationship between Timothy Mouse and Dumbo is cemented. We then overhear the circus master concocting another act for the Big Top, this one a "pyramid of pachyderms." When Timothy Mouse sneaks underneath the tent flap and whispers into the circus master's ear, there is **conflict with the situation.**

Chapter 9: "A Pyramid of Pachyderms"

Further establishment of the insensitivity of the circus master as he announces the pyramid of pachyderms in a Big Top show. When Dumbo runs out to the springboard, he trips over his ears. Again, **the conflict is with the situation.** As Dumbo tumbles into the ball and topples the pyramid, the resulting calamity and bedlam remind me of the comic payoff in the "Squirrelly in the Diner" chapter of Brad Bird's *The Iron Giant*. It is also a pretty classic Charlie Chaplin kind of moment. **Comedy is a factor of a character's limitations, which is why Dumbo's ears are funny.**

Chapter 10: "Dumbo's Disgrace"

Dumbo experiences shame and embarrassment when he is used as a circus clown. He also feels fear when he is forced to jump off the burning tower into the net below. **Audiences only empathize with emotion and, in this case, the emotion is fear.** We feel **sympathy** (literally, "feeling for") for Dumbo, but we also feel a lot of **empathy** (literally, "feeling into"). Timothy Mouse subsequently tries to cheer him up. By the end of the sequence, Dumbo is perfectly miserable and in tears. **Conflict with the situation.**

Chapter 11: "Dumbo Visits His Mother"

This is one of the most famous animation sequences of all time. Study it carefully. The acting is wonderful. No dialogue passes between Dumbo and his mother, and there is no side narration from Timothy Mouse. We are left to watch mother and child try to touch one another even though they can't see one another. **Note how much emotion there is in this exchange.** Their trunks touch and entwine lovingly. The action on both parts is to touch, and the obstacle is with the situation.

Chapter 12: "Dumbo Gets the Hiccups"

This is a fun and expository sequence. The animators had to get Dumbo, a baby after all, drunk and still make it all seem harmless. The acting lesson would be in the way that Timothy Mouse and Dumbo react to the champagne. Neither of them has ever been drunk before so they don't know anything about trying to preserve their dignity while drunk. They are simply taken along for an alcoholic ride. **Note the relaxation in their bodies and the shifting power centers. When you get drunk, the power center in your body becomes unstable. That is why you may stumble and sway.**

Chapter 13: "Pink Elephants on Parade"

This is a colorful, big-orchestra, extended *Fantasia*-like sequence and there is very little acting involved. The humor is based on improbability and morphing (elephant trunks turn into trumpets; elephants turn different colors . . .). It's the kind of lovely stuff that we no longer see in animated features.

Chapter 14: "Up a Tree"

We meet the crows (animation director: Ward Kimble). Once Dumbo and Timothy wake up and realize they are up a tree, they both have conflict with the situation. **Dumbo's action is to hang on and not fall. The obstacle is gravity. In any negotiation, there is a way to win and a way to lose. If he can regain his balance in the tree, he wins; if he falls, he loses.** He falls, of course. Remember, comedy has to do with the character's limitations. I personally love the acting in this sequence. The crows are fully realized characters.

Chapter 15: "When I See an Elephant Fly"

The crows perform a show-stopping musical number in which they mock Dumbo for thinking maybe he can fly. The sequence is exuberant and fun and good-natured. It's just a marvelous showpiece. After the singing stops, Timothy Mouse shames the crows for having made fun of poor Dumbo. The crows shed tears of empathy, and we know for sure they are going to be friends.

Chapter 16: "Dumbo Flies"

The crows give Dumbo a "magic feather"/placebo and shove him off a cliff. Dumbo's initial emotion is fear as he approaches the precipice. Once in the air, the emotion changes to happiness and delight. **Emotion tends to lead to action.**

Chapter 17: "Dumbo's Surprise"

Back under the Big Top, Dumbo is dressed as a clown and once again poised to jump from the burning building into the net below. This time the perch is several times higher than it was last time, creating the possibility of real danger. As Dumbo plunges toward earth, he drops the magic feather. Timothy Mouse slides to the end of Dumbo's trunk and pleads with him to spread his ears and fly even without the magic feather. The acting note is that **emotion tends to lead to action.** Dumbo is falling rapidly. If he will not fly, he will likely die. The stakes could not be higher. **It is an adrenaline moment.** That is why Timothy Mouse is so agitated. When Dumbo narrowly avoids disaster and soars into the air above the circus audience, we feel relief and joy. **In acting terms, it is a dramatic moment because it deals with the character's possibilities—rather than limitations—in life.** Then Dumbo gets back at all the people and animals that have made fun of him. They are caused to trip, fall in buckets of water, go tumbling, and so on. At this point, it is they who have the conflict with the situation, not Dumbo. They are acting to protect themselves and the conflict is that Dumbo is on their case.

The final sequence in which the circus train moves on to the next town simply ties up the theme in a nice package. The underdog has prevailed. Lesson learned.

3. Pinocchio

Walt Disney Home Video (1940)

Directors: Hamilton Luske, Ben Sharpsteen

Writing Credits: Carlo Collodi (novel *The Adventures of Pinocchio*), Aurelius Battaglia (story adaptation), William Cottrell (story adaptation), Otto Englander (story adaptation), Erdman Penner (story adaptation), Joseph Sabo (story adaptation), Ted Sears (story adaptation), Webb Smith (story adaptation)

Animators: Frank Thomas, Ollie Johnston, Milt Kahl (Pinocchio), Art Babbitt (Geppetto), Ward Kimball (Jiminy Cricket), Bill Tytla and Bob Stokes (Geppetto), Bill Tytla (lead Stromboli), Fred Moore (Lampwick), Norm Ferguson (Honest John and Gideon)

Voice Cast: Mel Blanc (hiccup sound effect), Don Brodie (Barker), Walter Catlett (J. Worthington Foulfellow), Frankie Darro (Lampwick), Cliff Edwards (Jiminy Cricket), Dickie Jones (Pinocchio), Charles Judels (Stromboli/The Coachman), Christian Rub (Geppetto), Evelyn Venable (The Blue Fairy)

The Blue Fairy was rotoscoped by Jack Campbell.

Overview

The character of Pinocchio appeals because he is such a typical little boy. You could almost replace him with Mickey Mouse and get the same effect. When he is excited, he is very excited, and when he is afraid, he is terrified. He acts impulsively most of the time, just like a young boy might be expected to do. It is easy to empathize with Pinocchio because his every move is clearly motivated by emotion.

Michael Barrier makes an astute observation in his book *Hollywood Cartoons: American Animation in Its Golden Age* (Oxford University Press, 1999): "The question before Disney had been, should he try to find some way to make Pinocchio likable as a puppet, or should he try to make him likable by making him less of a puppet and more of a boy?" (p. 239).

Analysis

Chapter 1: Opening Credits

Chapter 2: "One Night, a Long Time Ago"

Jiminy Cricket struggles with the oversized book. This gives a small amount of conflict to a scene that is basically just exposition. Very clever. You always want your character to *do* something. If Jiminy had not had to struggle with the book, he would have just stood there and talked to the camera. The cover is as heavy as a garage door to the little cricket, and the page is like a giant sheet. Ask yourself if you would have thought to add conflict by having him struggle with the page.

Note that the first time we see Pinocchio as a lifeless puppet, he has no eyebrows. It is significant that the animator left the eyebrows for last because they are one of the most expressive elements of the human face.

Chapter 3: "Little Wooden Head"

Geppetto gives Pinocchio his name. This involves zero conflict and is expository. **Jiminy Cricket gets caught in the internal mechanism of a clock and almost gets crushed. Low-grade conflict with situation.** It is interesting to me that the production team tried to put a bit of conflict into each scene, even if it is not major and doesn't have much to do with anything.

Chapter 4: "Geppetto's Wish"

Figaro the cat has fairly constant conflict with his situation in that he is trying to go to sleep and Geppetto continually interrupts him. Geppetto himself has zero conflict. Once Figaro and Geppetto are settled down, the conflict switches over to Jiminy Cricket, who cannot get to sleep for the noise of the clocks.

Chapter 5: "The Blue Fairy"

The Blue Fairy was a straightforward rotoscope and is therefore the weakest character in the movie, in my opinion.

Chapter 6: "Give a Little Whistle"

Jiminy, newly anointed "Sir Jiminy Cricket," the official conscience for Pinocchio, attempts a father-son advice session. **He hems and haws, the same as most fathers do when they try to give advice. This is conflict with the situation. It resolves itself when he starts singing the advice in the song, "Give a Little Whistle."** Suddenly, he has no doubt at all and becomes as graceful as Fred Astaire.

Chapter 7: "A Wish Come True"

Gepetto is frightened by a noise. He lights a candle, gets his pistol, and searches for prowlers. **Acting-wise, I can quibble with the degree of hand tremble, although I understand the tremble is intended to set up the upcoming gag. In life, a nervous person will act to** *control* **a tremble.** Geppetto is clearly unaccustomed to using the gun to defend himself. It is big and heavy and is an accident waiting to happen.

The gag happens when Pinocchio says, "Here I am!", scaring the cat, who jumps up Geppetto's nightgown, which in turn scares Geppetto into firing his pistol. This is a very funny sequence. It reminds me of the circus sequence in *Dumbo* when the elephant tries unsuccessfully to participate in the Big Top act. One event triggers a series of other events. **The trick to this kind of gag is that each of the resulting events must, in hindsight, be utterly logical.**

Geppetto cannot believe that the puppet has come to life. **This is an adrenaline moment for the old guy.** I like the choice of dousing himself with water. There were a lot of possible acting choices in that moment. People pinch themselves, for example, when they want to test if they are dreaming. Dousing himself with water was comic because it was so extreme. **Comedy is drama extended, elevated, exaggerated.** In a sense, the bucket of water can be seen as an extension and elevation of a simple pinch.

Pinocchio sets his own finger on fire and doesn't realize there is a problem. This establishes that he is not fully a human boy yet and it triggers an interesting empathetic response in the audience. Think about it: **When you see someone burn herself, don't you jump with alarm? That is because you empathize** with the feeling of being burned. When Pinocchio sets his finger on fire, your first impulse is to empathize, but the puppet himself does not react! This immediately signals that he is not yet human. Even if he didn't know it was wrong, a human boy would have felt the pain. Instead, the finger on fire provides conflict for Geppetto, who has to spring into action to save the puppet.

At the end of the sequence, Cleo the fish has **conflict with the situation** because Geppetto and Pinocchio have turned her water smoky.

Chapter 8: "Off to School"

Note how Pinocchio is jumping around with excitement and how he skips rather than walking or running when he heads off for school. **Emotion tends to lead to action.** We empathize with him a lot in this sequence. **This is also an adrenaline moment for Pinocchio. He will never forget his first day of school, especially because this is the day he meets Honest John and Gideon.**

Chapter 9: "Honest John and Gideon"

Note the peculiar walk rhythm of Honest John and Gideon. It is step-hold-step-hold-step-hold. Very interesting. The walk itself is creepy and sneaky, so we have a feeling about these characters almost from the instant they appear on screen. When Pinocchio goes skipping past in the opposite direction, the contrast between the two styles of walking is marked. Pinocchio is innocent, while Honest John and Gideon are stealthy.

Chapter 10: "Pinocchio Is Led Astray"

Pinocchio first has **conflict with the situation** when Honest John trips him with the cane. At the point where Pinocchio says he is going to school and attempts to leave, **the conflict switches to conflict with another character.** The conflict is resolved when Pinocchio starts dancing down the street with the bad guys. Remember, **a scene is a negotiation and, in any negotiation, there must be a way to win and a way to lose.** In this one, Pinocchio loses when he joins Honest John, but he doesn't yet realize it.

Pinocchio's decision to go with Honest John at the beginning of the song "An Actor's Life for Me" is interesting. Play it a couple of times and look closely. Pinocchio does not make a clear decision to accompany the fox and, in fact, appears doubtful until the song begins. Really, more than making a career decision, he is joining a fun dance. At this point, Honest John and Pinocchio's gaits are in sync. They both march in time with the same music. **Pinocchio's transition springs totally from emotion, not from a conceptual thinking process. If he stopped to think about what he was doing, he probably wouldn't do it.** Pinocchio in fact hasn't a clue what an actor is, what fame is, or any of that. He's just happy to go along.

Jiminy Cricket's entrance is on the run. He's "late the first day" and he's trying to catch up with Pinocchio. **Conflict with situation.** The next acting principle here happens when Jiminy is surprised by Pinocchio dancing off with Honest John and Gideon. **Play an action until something happens to make you play a different action.**

Gideon hits Honest John on the head with a mallet for a wonderful, classic cartoon gag. What I like most about this sequence is the way that Gideon reacts after he has hit Honest John. First he runs away. He knows he is in deep trouble. Then he returns and tries to figure how to get Honest John unstuck from his stovetop hat. The gag would have been a little stronger if Gideon's thought process was a bit clearer. **Indecision is actually a series of tiny decisions and changes of mind.** Gideon appears generally perplexed, but he is actually making decisions about how to proceed. His choice becomes clear when he starts trying to pry the hat off Honest John's head and then uses the mallet again.

Chapter 11: "I've Got No Strings"

This is Pinocchio's first real introduction to cruelty in life. Stromboli hits him on the head after he trips in the opening moments of his song, "I've Got No Strings." It is a violent blow, too, made all the more so because Pinocchio is such an innocent. We see his look of surprise (**acting is reacting**), but before that can translate into real fear, Stromboli realizes that there is no financial gain in mistreating the puppet in public. He turns on a dime and acts friendly again, and Pinocchio—ever the trusting soul—immediately gets back into the swing of the party.

The action shifts back to Geppetto and his search for the lost Pinocchio. **Conflict with situation.** You can also see a lot of sadness in the droop of Geppetto's body as he is putting on his coat to go search for the boy. **Sadness will tend to make a character feel heavier.**

Chapter 12: "Pinocchio Taken Prisoner"

Cheap gag involving garlic breath. Stromboli eats half a garlic clove and then brings Pinocchio's face close to his own. Pinocchio's eyes water. I could have lived without it, to be truthful. **I think gags should come from the logic of the scene.**

Until the very moment that Stromboli locks Pinocchio in the birdcage, the puppet is trusting. Even as Stromboli carries him to the cage, Pinocchio is laughing, thinking this is all a fun game. The transition comes when Pinocchio realizes his true awful situation. This is where he comes face-to-face with cruelty and recognizes it for what it is. **He wants to escape. He has conflict with another character and also conflict with the situation.**

There is a wonderful tension-building moment when Gepetto comes within feet of the captive Pinocchio in the rain.

He calls out into the night, "Pino—", but the last part of the puppet's name is drowned out by thunder. If it had not thundered at that moment, Jiminy and Pinocchio would have heard Gepetto, and the story would have come to a different and much earlier conclusion.

Chapter 13: "The Blue Fairy Comes to Pinocchio's Aid"

This is an interesting and important sequence because it is the first time we see Pinocchio in conflict with himself, which is a hallmark of humanity. Up until this point, the conflict has been either with the situation or with another character. **An element of human maturity is the ability to tell right from wrong.** Pinocchio lies to the Blue Fairy and his nose starts growing. He keeps lying, choosing with each lie to lie some more. At each step, he has the choice of telling the truth. Finally, when his nose is fully distended, he is ashamed and vows to be truthful from now on. This is a key moment in Pinocchio's journey from being a puppet.

In the final moment of this chapter, after Jiminy and Pinocchio have escaped, Pinocchio calls out loudly and happily, "Goodbye, Mister Stromboli!" I don't like that moment because it not logical and it was unnecessary. Pinocchio surely knows that Stromboli is a bad guy at this point, and he would be smart enough not to call out to him. The objective in the sequence is to escape. Calling out like that compromises the negotiation and makes Pinocchio appear rather stupid.

Chapter 14: "The Coachman's Proposition"

This sequence is interesting to watch because we have a new character and a change of atmosphere, but when you look underneath, there is not much going on. The cigar jokes take up a lot of space. When the Coachman mentions Pleasure

Island, it is confusing that Honest John and Gideon have such a shocked and fearful reaction. It doesn't make sense, if you stop to think about it, because we have established by this point in the story that these guys have zero scruples. As the sequence ends, it seems that Honest John and Gideon will be unwilling accomplices to the kidnapping of Pinocchio. Why should they be unwilling? They will, after all, be well paid and, up until now, they have had no problem with selling Pinocchio down the river.

Chapter 15: "Honest John Waylays Pinocchio Again"

Pinocchio has conflict/negotiation with another character, Honest John. Significantly, Honest John and Gideon literally lift Pinocchio off the ground and carry him off to the boat. **The puppet is thereby relieved of the necessity to resolve the conflict.** I wish that Pinocchio had been allowed to stick with the conflict with another character and then be carried to the boat calling out for Jiminy. This would have played out stronger in the next sequence when Pinocchio first meets Lampwick. The sequence has Pinocchio repeatedly attempting to explain to Lampwick that the ace of spades Honest John gave him is a "boat ticket." It would have worked better, in my opinion, if Pinocchio were doubtful and fearful about this new journey. After all, he does not know that Jiminy is riding underneath the wagon. All he really knows is that he is alone and going to some new and maybe fearful place. It would have been effective storytelling to allow him to be afraid.

Chapter 16: "Pleasure Island"

This is the first time we see Pinocchio eat anything. He eats pie and ice cream. Humans eat; puppets don't. Though it would not register on the average movie viewer, this bit of business helps establish that Pinocchio is now much more human than puppet.

When Pinocchio says it is "fun to be bad," you get the sense that he really doesn't know what "bad" means. I wish he had been allowed a decisive moment where he makes a clear choice to do a bad thing. For example, Lampwick tosses a brick through a beautiful stained-glass window. It would have been nice if Pinocchio had also picked up a brick, hesitated (conflict with self), and then tossed his brick, too, through a pretty window.

Chapter 17: "Later That Night"

Pinocchio has conflict with the situation when he smokes the cigar.

Jiminy has indirect conflict with another character, namely Lampwick. He loses that negotiation and heads for the boat. **Play an action until something happens to make you play a different action.** Jiminy sees the Coachman rounding up boys who have turned into jackasses, and he immediately changes course, returning to save Pinocchio from an awful fate.

This is a wonderful sequence because it is nightmarish. A psychiatrist told me once that **the difference between a dream and a nightmare is that nightmares deal with mortality.** When the boys turn into jackasses, they lose their ability to function as humans. In other words, if they live as jackasses, they perish as humans. Nightmare. Excellent storytelling, particularly since the target audience for this movie is young.

Chapter 18: "Lampwick Makes a Jackass of Himself"

Pinocchio, watching Lampwick turn into a jackass at the pool table, first decides not to drink beer and then, separately, not to smoke any more cigars. It is late in the game, but he is making choices.

Pinocchio's reaction to Lampwick's transformation is illogical. He laughs on the line, "You sure do!" and then brays like a jackass. I can see why it was done this way. The animator wanted to set up the transformation from laugh to braying. Still, the reaction is an illogical progression from what transpired only moments earlier. Pinocchio decided not to smoke or drink, and at least part of the decision was based on fear. The logical extension would have been more fear. Anyway, it would be terrifying—not funny—to see your friend turn into a jackass right before your eyes.

As Lampwick becomes 100 percent jackass, Pinocchio is wrenched with fear. This is logical and right. The sequence is brilliant and terrifying, full of emotion. **I very much like it that Lampwick kicks and bucks in his resistance to being a jackass. Humans act to survive. His conversion into a jackass is a conversion into death.** It helps create in the audience a sense of empathy when he fights the transformation so much.

By this point, Pinocchio is scared out of his wits and he has **extreme conflict with the situation.** Jiminy's arrival resolves that conflict as he leads Pinocchio to safety.

Chapter 19: "Sad Homecoming"

Conflict with the situation as Pinocchio discovers Geppetto is gone. Then comes the message, presumably from the Blue Fairy, explaining about Monstro the whale.

Pinocchio, now functioning as a human, immediately opts for saving Geppetto from the whale. He has zero concern for his own safety. His priority is to save his father. This would not, by the way, be altruistic behavior. Pinocchio would probably not want to live knowing that his father was dead.

At this point, we could also say that Pinocchio becomes a hero. **A hero is an ordinary person who overcomes great odds or a great enemy to achieve a positive goal.**

30

Chapter 20: "The Undersea Search for Geppetto"

This totally illogical underwater sequence goes on far too long before Pinocchio finally winds up face to face with Geppetto. I suppose the storytellers wanted to have some fun with the underwater fishy environment, but the whole thing doesn't make much sense. Why doesn't he drown?

The sequence with Geppetto in the whale's belly is exposition. He has conflict with his situation, but there isn't much he can do about it. Therefore, it is not a real negotiation.

Chapter 21: "Monstro Awakens"

This is an extended action sequence. Lovely animation, not much going on performance-wise. Pinocchio tries to escape Monstro's gaping and hungry mouth. Meanwhile, Geppetto finally has some fish to eat in the whale's belly.

Chapter 22: "A Soggy Reunion"

Pinocchio is capable of abstract thought, another hallmark of humans. He figures out how to make the whale sneeze! Even Geppetto, theoretically the brighter and wiser, doesn't think of that.

Chapter 23: "A Whale of a Sneeze"

Magnificent action sequences as the whale sneezes and chases Pinocchio and Geppetto. The conflict is obvious. This is a wonderfully tumultuous event, and it perfectly sets up the ending of total stillness as we learn that Pinocchio may have drowned.

Pinocchio is a true hero now. He has overcome the odds and saved his father's life.

Chapter 24: "The Dream Fulfilled"

Pinocchio is on his deathbed, lifeless. Geppetto, Figaro, Cleo, and Jiminy mourn. Then the Blue Fairy carries out her side of the deal, bringing the puppet to life—as a real boy.

Emotion tends to lead to action. Everybody celebrates. Jiminy has a quiet moment with the Wishing Star—I mean, Blue Fairy—outside. The End; music up.

4. Treasure Planet

Walt Disney Pictures (2002)

Producer: Roy Conli

Directors: Ron Clements, John Musker

Writing Credits: Ken Harsha (story), Barry Johnson (story supervisor), Kaan Kalyon (story), Mark Kennedy (story), Sam Levine (story), Donnie Long (story), Frank Nissen (story), Terry Rossio (costory), Robert Louis Stevenson (novel *Treasure Island*)

Animators: Mark Austin (animator B.E.N.), Noreen Beasley (rough inbetweener Amelia and Scroop), Nancy Beiman (supervising animator Billy Bones), Doug Bennett (animator B.E.N.), Bill Berg (clean-up co-lead John Silver), Eric Daniels (CGI lead animator John Silver), Ken Duncan (supervising animator Captain Amelia and Scroop), Eric Gervais-Despres (scene planner), T. Daniel Hofstedt (supervising animator Mister Arrow), Glen Keane (supervising animator John Silver), Vera Lanpher (clean-up supervisor), Karen Lundeen (clean-up colead John Silver), John Musker (developer), Sergio Pablos (supervising animator Dr. Doppler), John Ripa (lead character animator Jim Hawkins), Marc Smith (animator John Silver), Mike Show (animator Morph), Oskar Urretabizkaia (supervising animator B.E.N.), Kevin Waldvogel (animator), Dean Wellins (animator)

Art Director: Andy Gaskill

Voice Cast: Roscoe Lee Browne (Arrow), Cory Burton (Onus), Dane Davis (Morph), Joseph Gordon-Levitt (Jim Hawkins), Tony Jay (Narrator), Austin Majors (Young Jim), Patrick McGoohan (Billy Bones), Michael McShane (Hands), Laurie Metcalf (Sarah Hawkins), Brian Murray (John Silver), David Hyde Pierce (Delbert Doppler), Martin Short (B.E.N.), Emma Thompson (Captain Amelia), Michael Wincott (Scroop)

Overview

Treasure Planet is what Hollywood calls a high-concept film. The pitch session behind it can be summed up as "*Treasure Island* meets *Star Wars*." High concept often succeeds at the box office, but this time it did not, even in the hands of a stellar production team and tens of millions of dollars in Disney promotion.

There has been plenty of industry debate about what went wrong with *Treasure Planet*. Without any doubt, it is a drop-dead beautiful movie to watch, with those nineteenth-century ocean ships cruising through outer space.

My personal view is that the concept pitched better than it executed. The single most troubling issue is the way that some of the leading characters from Stevenson's original *Treasure Island* are converted into aliens. Aliens in movies are tricky in the first place because we humans empathize with other humans. If you want an audience to empathize with an alien, you have to humanize him so that we can relate to him emotionally. When a storyteller announces that a character on screen is 80 percent human and 20 percent dog, which is the case of Delbert Doppler, we in the audience are already scratching our heads a bit. As we move through the chapters of the DVD, I will point out where I think the problems arise. Many readers will disagree with me, I suspect, but I hope my take on the movie at least encourages discussion.

The DVD of *Treasure Planet* includes an invaluable visual commentary that I think is essential viewing for readers of this book. The producer, codirectors, and various key animators explain what they were trying to accomplish and how things evolved during production. Given that the movie ultimately does not work very well, it is useful to keep those visual commentary observations in mind.

Analysis

Chapter 1: Opening Credits/ "A Young Boy's Dream"

According to the visual commentary, the prologue sequence that appears in the movie was added late in production, evidently after some test screenings. Hollywood studios are very fond of test screenings. The problem with them is that the filmmakers may begin to distrust their own best judgment about what will work and what won't, and they will try to adjust the movie to get the best test numbers. Test screenings for *Treasure Planet* indicated that the audience found the original opening "too dark," and so they came up with this new, sweeter, more Disney-esque prologue. The original opening sequence is fortunately included on the DVD under "Deleted Scenes." For my money, the way they had it in the first place was much stronger than what they wound up with after test screenings. The current prologue is a flashback bedtime sequence that introduces Jim Hawkins as a young child. In it, we learn that he is a typical boy with a bigger-than-life imagination and has a loving relationship with his mother, Sarah. In terms of acting and scene construction, the movement and behavior of the two characters works fine, but the scene is 100 percent exposition. It lacks negotiation. Also, I think it would have been nice to have Jim's father stick his head in the room at some point. Throughout the movie, the father is something of a mystery figure. If we had a glimpse into the son's love for his father, then the father's eventual disappearance would have more impact. This bedtime scene probably was the best opportunity to introduce that character. Instead, the entire scene involves only mother and son.

There are two much larger problems with this prologue though. First, because of the cozy bedroom setting, the audience understandably thinks the action is taking place on Earth, maybe in the nineteenth century. In fact, Jim and his mom are on the planet Montressor some time in the distant future. Second, the audience is led to believe that the entire concept of a planet that contains hidden treasure is an idea from a child's storybook. It is fodder for a bedtime story. It will not be until Chapter 3 that the audience learns the treasure is real! In my view, therefore, the prologue as it is presented muddies the story at a time when the audience is forming initial impressions. It is beautifully animated of course but, in terms of story development, it puts a burden on the audience to unscramble events, characters, and time frame in Chapter 3.

Flashback is a risky and often overused device for storytelling anyway. Robert McKee offers a useful perspective on this in his invaluable book *Story, Substance, Structure, Style, and the Principles of Screenwriting* (HarperCollins 1997, pp. 341–43). Though I have seen flashback work successfully many times in movies, I still very much prefer that a story be exposed in a linear ongoing fashion.

The action then shifts to "twelve years later" when fifteen-year-old James is hot-rodding on his solar-board. **There are no real negotiations of any kind in this opening chapter.** The boy has a bit of conflict with his situation because he wants to read his book rather than go to sleep and, later as a teenager, he has conflict with his situation because he is risking his life by driving too fast. Overall, however, there is nothing dramatically going on in the first chapter. The solar-board sequence is straightforward video game stuff. It's not really a structured scene, and it goes on too long. Significantly, this too was added late in production, along with the new prologue.

Chapter 2: "The Warning"

A basic tenet of effective screenwriting is "Show. Don't tell." In this chapter, the storytellers unfortunately do a lot of telling. When the robot-police bring Jim home, we learn from their conversation with his upset mother that the boy has a history of truancy and is on probation. After the cops leave, Jim goes off to sit on the roof and sulk and we get more expository information from an eavesdropped conversation between Sarah and Dr. Delbert Doppler. They talk about how Jim's father "left" when he was young and how he has been unsettled ever since. This information is important! Ideally, it would have been delivered within a structured scene that involved conflict, negotiation, and resolution. It is not enough that the characters are generally upset and unhappy.

In the visual commentary, the producer and directors use the word "sympathy" when talking about building feeling into a character. **There is a big difference between sympathy and empathy**, and I frequently hear knowledgeable people in the animation industry get them mixed up. **Sympathy literally means "feeling for" and empathy literally means "feeling into." You as an animator want to generate a sense of empathy—not sympathy—in the audience.** You'll gain empathy when the character acts to survive. In this sequence, Jim goes to sit on the roof and sulk, and we feel sorry for him. Sympathy instead of empathy. He overhears his mother telling Dr. Doppler about his troubled childhood. The visual commentary explains that the initial idea was to leave Jim out of the scene altogether, but it was decided it would build "sympathy" for him if he overheard his mother talking. The directors decided that the conversation between Sarah and Dr. Doppler would play best if it was reflected in Jim's face. It seems to me the scene would have played better if we had either stayed in the room with Sarah and Dr. Doppler or, even more preferable, if the scene had been written in a way that included Jim in the actual dialogue. It doesn't help things to establish him this early in the movie as depressed and passive.

Regarding the character design of Delbert Doppler, supervising animator Sergio Pablos explains in visual commentary that Doppler was first conceived as 100 percent human, but the decision was made to try something more extreme. He came up with a way that Doppler—an alien—could be 80 percent human and 20 percent dog. He figured that would help establish that the action takes place somewhere in the distant future. I appreciate his logic, but the dog ears bothered me for the entire movie because I couldn't figure how it worked in an evolutionary sense. At what point did humans start mating with dogs? Maybe it was a cloning experiment gone awry? Later in the movie, Doppler will mate with the very feline Captain Amelia (also an alien), and they will have a baby. Given that she is 20 percent cat and Doppler is 20 percent dog, what does all of this mean for interspecies evolution? The bottom line for me is, I wish they had stuck with their original conception of Dr. Doppler (and Captain Amelia) as 100 percent human. If they wanted to make these characters more interesting, there were myriad ways to do it in terms of character development.

The arrival of Billy Bones, the turtlelike character who is hiding the map of Treasure Planet, is a strong plot point and swings the action forward. Jim rushes from his roof perch to help pull Billy Bones from his wrecked ship. **The physical** action is motivated by emotion, and it works. The action is to pull the man out to safety; the objective is to save his life. The obstacle is that the ship might blow up or something. **Conflict with the situation.**

The marauding space pirates charge in, ransacking and burning the Denbow Inn to the ground. This is a visually dazzling sequence but doesn't offer much in terms of scene structure. We learn that the pirates are bad guys. Jim, Sarah, and Delbert have to escape out the back in order to save their lives. It would have been nice if, say, Jim had tried to save a favorite picture of his dad. Then we would have learned something about his character and feelings.

Chapter 3: "Jim's Quest"

The action takes place in Dr. Doppler's observatory. The place is opulent, which establishes that the Doctor has enough money to finance the upcoming expedition to Treasure Planet.

Jim accidentally opens the spherical map to Treasure Planet. This sequence contains visual delights but is mainly expository. We learn about the solar system and also that the characters are not on earth but on the planet Montressor.

When Delbert points out the position of Treasure Planet on the map, we in the audience have to figure out if Treasure Planet is a real place or something from a child's storybook, which is what we were led to believe in the Chapter 1 bedtime sequence. This is confusing storytelling.

When Jim announces that "this is the answer to all our problems," he begins to negotiate with his mother (**conflict with another person**) about whether he can go on the journey to find the treasure. It's a confusing negotiation, though, because she is actually arguing that Jim has lost his mind. Her contention is that Treasure Planet doesn't exist at all. According to her, the boy is confusing fantasy with reality. Is Jim really crazy? Was Treasure Planet just a boy's storybook bedtime thing? Did his father's departure send Jim totally off the deep end? Are we really lost in space? The acting is good in this sequence, but the writing is weak. We should not, here in Chapter 3, be debating whether or not Treasure Planet actually exists. Much of the problem springs from the changed prologue.

In terms of performance, both Jim and Delbert get excited by the discovery on the map and begin jumping around in anticipation of a grand adventure and super riches. **Emotion tends to lead to action.** But once again there is no negotiation. **The character movement is justified in emotional terms, but the scene lacks structure.** Delbert, meanwhile, keeps talking about what a brilliant scientist he is, but the evidence on-screen is that he would have difficulty draining the bathtub. In the visual narration, we learn that the little dance Delbert does ("Go, Delbert! Go, Delbert! Go, Delbert!") originated as an ad lib by the voice actor, David Hyde Pierce. They kept it in because they thought it was cute. It is cute, but I think it makes the character seem unduly silly—especially since in the next chapter we are expected to believe that he is organized enough to have hired the entire crew of the RLS *Legacy.*

Chapter 4: "The RLS *Legacy*"

We see the spaceport for the first time. It is a visually exciting place and we get a glimpse of some wonderful space creatures. For some reason, Delbert is wearing a space suit, but nobody else is. Why? If they don't really need suits, then this is a wasted bit of gag. **For Jim, arrival at the spaceport would be an adrenaline moment.**

The flatulent alien character is an excuse for potty humor and doesn't contribute anything to the story.

We discover that the captain of the R.L.S. *Legacy* is a super-competent alien female (80 percent human, 20 percent cat). That's fine, except that we soon learn that she did not hire her own crew—Delbert did. My reaction is that, based on Delbert's character development so far, he is too inept to have hired the crew.

Captain Amelia is, according to the bonus extras narration, based on a cat. The animators tried explicitly to make her behave in a catlike way, and yet they wanted her to be 80 percent human. That is a good idea, but there is a trap in it. Cats don't show a lot of facial emotion or reaction. They do what they do and are very independent souls. It is hard to know how Captain Amelia feels most of the time.

Chapter 5: "John Silver"

Jim and Delbert meet the cyborg John Silver. There is immediate tension between Jim and John Silver, but it does not manifest itself as a negotiation. John Silver casts sneaky glances at Jim and is seemingly up to no good. He is physically powerful and can do terrible things with his mechanical arm. We also meet the character Morph. In the visual narration, someone says that Morph is "all feelings and no intellect." Though I appreciate the intent, the fact is that **feelings (emotions) are automatic value responses. You can't have "feelings and no intellect." It is a contradiction.** This particular character will morph playfully into this or that object all through the rest of the movie, but it does not display any emotional range until the very end of the movie, when it has to decide whether to go with John Silver or stay with Jim. It is an inhuman thing, not empathetic. The main function it seems to provide is to be a sounding board for John Silver and Jim from time to time. If Morph were not there, they'd be talking to themselves.

Chapter 6: "Setting Sail"

Let's talk for a minute about Captain Amelia. Note that she is very cerebral. That is a perfectly fine quality for a ship captain, but we have the challenge of establishing empathy for her. **Humans empathize with emotion.** Dr. Doppler is also an alien, but he displays more emotional range than Amelia. I would, for example, like to know how she feels about being a ship captain. One opportunity would be when the ship accelerates into space and she advises Doppler, "Brace yourself, doctor." It would have been effective to have another shot of her, maybe a medium close-up that would allow us to see emotion. Does she enjoy the sensation of sailing? Does it thrill her? Is she in her element? Where was she born? How did she come to be a captain in what is obviously a man's domain? There are zero other female characters of any significance in the movie except for Jim's mother, Sarah, and she is pretty traditional. Captain Amelia is an important character on several levels, and the movie would have profited by allowing us insights into her value system and emotional life.

I like the shot of Jim as he gazes in wonder at the space whales. The sight of them makes him happy. Note his expression. Notice that his happiness makes you empathize with the character and feel happy, too.

After John Silver tosses Mr. Mop and Mrs. Bucket into Jim's hands, Jim goes into a kind of sulk. He's angry, but the emotion is not leading to any action. **Acting is doing; it is not enough to simply convey feelings. Emotions alone carry zero theatrical currency.**

Jim gets into a physical confrontation with the lobsterlike Mr. Scroop. **Conflict with another character.** The problem is that Jim is purely a victim in the confrontation, and it falls to John Silver to rescue him. It would have been stronger if Jim, even while pinned to the mast by Mr. Scroop, had at least *tried* to free himself. He could have reached for a weapon or somehow acted to defend himself.

Chapter 7: "A Mutiny in the Making"

At the top of this chapter, John Silver conspires with his fellow pirates. **The room is full to the brim with colorful characters, and we do not care about any of them. Mainly, this is because they are aliens and do not have human-type emotion.** John Silver himself is an alien but, except for some fun he has with the mechanical arm, he behaves as 100 percent human throughout the movie, with a full spectrum of human emotion. It seems to me that, in the case of John Silver, the 80/20 percent human/alien split is more like 95/05.

The action moves topside as we see Jim talking with Morph. This short sequence contributes nothing and could have been left out altogether. The visual narration says that the directors were ambivalent about including this in the first place. What we learn is that Jim is tired of mopping, and Morph can turn into various forms, including a miniature imitation of Mr. Scroop. But we already knew that about Morph. The sequence could have started instead with John Silver's entrance up the stairs.

If you are going to add gags to a sequence, ask yourself if the information being communicated is useful to the story. Charlie Chaplin had plenty of gags in his movies, as did Mack Sennett's Keystone Kops. There are very good reasons why Chaplin became legendary while the Keystone Kops faded away. **A gag is not in itself going to carry a whole lot of voltage if it isn't hooked into character development and story.**

The scene between John Silver and Jim is well acted, but the structure is weak. We have already established that Jim does not like John Silver. On what basis do we now get such an extreme change of heart? Why is Jim so easily persuaded to start telling John Silver about how his father abandoned him? It makes sense that Jim would be grateful to John Silver for having saved him from Scroop, but this much of a change strains credibility. It is one thing to be grateful and quite another to start sharing intimacies.

Chapter 8: "I'm Still Here" (Jim's Theme)

This is a transitional sequence in which Jim comes to see John Silver as a father figure. The negotiation is between characters, as John Silver is determined to exhaust Jim with manual labor on the ship, while Jim is determined not to be broken. The transitional point/resolution comes when John Silver observes Jim asleep and protectively places a jacket over him to keep him warm. In terms of performance, the transformation on John Silver's face is the strongest moment in the entire movie so far. It would have been nice if, after his transformation, we had a close-up shot of Jim reacting to the cozy coat.

Song: "I'm Still Here" by John Rzeznik of the Goo Goo Dolls.

This sequence refers back to the prologue.

Chapter 9: "A Star Gone Supernova"

The visual narration says that the directors and producers consider this scene in the boat to be some of the best acting in the movie, and I certainly agree. In the first place, it is well structured, which is a function of writing. Second, there are clear negotiations going on. John Silver and Jim are still negotiating the level of trust they will extend to one another, and we see a moment of real vulnerability in John Silver when he sadly observes that you sometimes "give up a few things when chasing a dream." When he moves from one end of the boat to the other and places his arm around Jim, the move is motivated by emotion. Acting-wise, the move is correct and meaningful. I suggest you play this sequence two or three times, focusing on the reaction shots. **Acting is doing, but it is also reacting. This excellent scene between Jim and John Silver is very much based on reaction.**

After that sequence, the remainder of the chapter is a long action sequence with few surprises and only adrenaline rushes. **(An adrenaline rush is quite different from an adrenaline moment.)** Everybody is trying to survive. Mister Scroop proves once again that he is a villain. Jim saves John Silver's life, thereby sealing their budding father-son relationship.

Chapter 10: "Getting in Too Deep"

After it is discovered that Mr. Arrow is missing, there is an opportunity to display a bit of emotional complexity in Captain Amelia. I would have liked to see her betray more sadness before she braces herself and instructs the crew to carry on. Her body could have sagged. Mr. Arrow was apparently her main friend on the ship, and the two of them evidently went back a long way together. His death was reason enough for a larger reaction from the captain. **A character's strength is often best exposed via small glimpses of vulnerability.** Someone in the visual narration says that there was at one time a scene in which Captain Amelia tearfully withdrew to her cabin, but they decided not to use it. They felt that the focus in the sequence should be on Jim, not Captain Amelia. I think they could have tried to have it both ways—with Captain Amelia and Jim both displaying emotional reaction.

The bonus extras narration says that the scene between John Silver and Jim is "a pivotal point in the movie." The father-and-son relationship is cemented. The problem with the scene, as I see it, is that when Jim cries out, "Don't you see? I screwed up!", he slumps once again into despair. That is not an empathetic acting choice. It generates sympathy rather than empathy. It would arguably have been stronger if Jim had tried to *do* something about the feeling he is experiencing. Slumping against the post is an emotional attitude, but it is not a strong acting choice. **Acting is doing. A scene is a negotiation.**

We do indeed have a negotiation when John Silver says, "Now you listen, James Hawkins. You have the makings of greatness in you. But you have to take the helm and chart your own course. Stick to it no matter the squalls. . . ." Will Jim accept the challenge and make something of himself? Or will he give up and spend the rest of his life as a loser? Acting-wise, this is a good moment. I wish that Jim were more defiant, more resistant, and more intent on a contrary course of action. Somebody decided to make him a passive recipient of John Silver's parental advice. It works, but the scene could have had more theatrical tension. For instance, after John Silver tells Jim that he has the makings of greatness in him, note that the next shot has Jim sort of buying into it. His expression says, "You think so . . . ?" It would have been stronger if the expression had been, "Screw you!" There needs to be a negotiation. He should not just roll over and accept John Silver's advice so easily. Note that he puts his head on Silver's stomach in the next shot. That move says, "I accept what you say. . . ." I think the negotiation never really takes flight, and there is no back-and-forth. Silver advises, and Jim accepts. Not enough.

Chapter 11: "Jim Hears the Truth"

The game of hide-and-seek with Morph is contrived and doesn't carry any emotional voltage. Its only evident purpose is to place

Jim within hearing distance of the conversation between John Silver and the other pirates.

Jim's reaction to the news that John Silver only cares about treasure is interesting but somehow not very moving. The problem is that Jim has not displayed much depth up to this point in the movie. If you are not very deep, you don't have far to sink.

When Jim grabs a knife and punctures John Silver's leg, his moves are motivated by emotion. Very good.

Chapter 12: "Protecting the Map"

The only acting moment of significance is when John Silver cannot bring himself to shoot Jim. **Conflict with self.** Internally, he's trying to decide if he's really a good guy or a bad guy. He prefers to be a bad guy, but his heart is saying he's a good guy.

Chapter 13: "B.E.N."

Jim meets B.E.N. (Bio Electronic Navigator), an alien character that has been marooned on this odd planet for a hundred years and has become loopy. **The character is amusing but is initially too frenetic and disjointed to empathize with. Robots don't have real emotion.** As I said earlier in this analysis, if you start out with a character being an alien, you have the challenge of somehow making him significant to the viewer. We empathize with emotion.

When B.E.N. asks Jim to make a pit stop at "my place," it is apparently so he can go to the bathroom. Do robots go to the bathroom? This looks like a bit of contrived business. I would have liked it better if he wanted to stop back home to get some oil for a squeaky hinge.

The captain finally—for the first time in the movie—shows a bit of vulnerability as she reacts to B.E.N.'s reference about her and Delbert being a romantic couple. She is falling in love with him. The audience is allowed to empathize with her at last.

Chapter 14: "Bargaining for the Map"

This is mainly another action sequence. The scene between Jim and John Silver doesn't go anywhere. At this point, Silver has bounced back and forth so much on the point of whether he is loyal to Jim or the treasure that we don't know what he thinks. Evidently he is coming down on the side of treasure. Jim's commitment to stand up to him is late in coming. In terms of scene construction, the negotiations are weak. What does Jim want from John Silver, especially knowing that only moments before, he was shooting bullets at him? Jim keeps hoping against hope that John Silver is his buddy, his new father, but all of the evidence says otherwise. Jim's persistence in believing only makes his character seem weaker.

Chapter 15: "Sneaking Back on Ship"

The fight between Jim and Scroop is frustrating. Morph saves Jim's life and, in the final moments of the conflict, Jim does not overcome Scroop. Instead, Scroop loses his balance and drifts off into space. It would have been more emotionally satisfying if Jim had more directly defeated Scroop. It would have better helped define Jim as a hero.

Chapter 16: "The Discovery"

After all of this long journey, the key to the opening of the map is left to coincidence. Jim is knocked on his hands and knees and, voila!, he accidentally comes upon the very spot where the map should be placed in order to magically open. This was too much coincidence for me to accept.

Chapter 17: "The Treasure"

Another terrific and compelling action sequence. At the ultimate moment, John Silver has to choose between treasure and saving Jim's life. Yes—no—yes—no. . . . **Ambivalence is played by making choices and then changing your mind.** In the end, John Silver chooses Jim over the treasure. By this point in the story, however, it is hard to give him a lot of points for morality. It seems as though he could have just as easily gone the other way and chosen the treasure. Of course that would have given the movie an unacceptable ending.

Chapter 18: "The Escape"

Action sequence.

Chapter 19: "Silver and Jim Say Good-bye"

Tearful and heartfelt good-bye between Jim and John Silver. The movement is motivated by emotion, but the sequences do not offer much in the way of negotiation.

Chapter 20: "Going Home/End Credits"

Jim comes home a hero, and his mom gives him a big hug. The captain and Delbert have evidently gotten married because they now have a baby with dog ears, just like Delbert. I suppose that dogs are the dominant gene when it comes to 20 percent cat versus 20 percent dog? Maybe the baby should also have had cat whiskers.

5. Monsters, Inc.

Pixar Animation Studios (2001)

Executive Producers: John Lasseter, Andrew Stanton

Producer: Darla K. Anderson

Associate Producer: Kori Rae

Directors: Pete Docter, David Silverman, Lee Unkrich

Screenwriters: Andrew Stanton, Daniel Gerson

Story: Pete Docter, Jill Culton, Jeff Pidgeon, Ralph Eggleston

Story Artists: Max Brace, Jim Capobianco, David Fulp, Rob Gibbs, Jason Katz, Bud Luckey, Matthew Luhn, Ted Mathot, Ken Mitchroney, Sanjay Patel, Jeff Pidgeon, Joe Ranft, Bob Scott, David Skelly, Nathan Stanton

Additional Storyboarding: Geefwee Boedoe, Joseph "Rocket" Ekers, Jorgen Klubien, Angus MacLane, Ricky Vega Nierva, Floyd Norman, Jan Pinkava

Animators: Scott Clark (directing animator), Rich Quade (supervising animator), Glenn McQueen (supervising animator), Doug Sweetland (directing animator), Kyle Balda, Alan Barillaro, Steven Barnes, Bobby Beck, Misha Berenstein, Dylan Brown, Brett Coderre, Tim Crawfurd, Ricardo Curtis, Dave Devan, Doug Dooley, Ike Feldman, Andrew Gordon, Stephen Gregory, Jimmy Hayward, Jesse Hollander, John Kahrs, Nancy Kato, Karen Kiser, Shawn P. Krause, Wendell Lee, Angus Maclane, Dan Mason, Amy McNamara, Jon Mead, Billy

Merritt, Dave Mullins, James Ford Murphy, Peter Nash, Victor Navone, Bret Parker, Michael Parks, Sanjay Patel, Bobby Podesta, Jeff Pratt, Bret Pulliam, Roger Rose, Robert H. Russ, Gini Cruz Santos, Andy Schmidt, Alan Sperling, Patty Kihm Stevenson, Ross Stevenson, David Tart, J. Warren Trezevant, Mike Venturini, Tasha Wedeen, Adam Wood, Kureha Yokoo, Ron Zoman

Voice Cast: John Goodman (James P. "Sulley" Sullivan), Billy Crystal (Mike Wazowski), Mary Gibbs (Boo), Steve Buscemi (Randall Boggs), James Coburn (Henry J. Waternoose), Jennifer Tilly (Celia), Bob Peterson (Roz), John Ratzenberger (Yeti), Frank Oz (Fungus), Dan Gerson (Needleman and Smitty)

Overview

Monsters, Inc. speaks to the power in a child's cries and the even greater power in a child's laughter. It is very shamanistic film-making, and I predict it will therefore find its place among the most classic of U.S. feature animation.

Analysis

Chapter 1: Opening Credits

Chapter 2: "Monster in the Closet"

We are in the training/simulation facility of Monsters, Inc., where monsters are taught how to scare children. Mr. Bile tries it but winds up scaring himself. This is a fun, well-constructed sequence because we do not at first realize we are in a simulator. I particularly like the way the way the animators build the kid's fear. The closet door creaks open, which causes him to experience fear. Emotion tends to lead to action, so he huddles down further under the covers and sneaks a glance at the closet door. The next cut to the closet door shows that what the kid sees is just a football jersey.

The sequence in which Mr. Bile falls on the jacks and careens around the room wrecking everything is marvelous. Again, **emotion tends to lead to action.** Bile scared the bejeezus out of himself! **Comedy is drama extended, heightened, oxygenated.** Bile could have simply fallen on the floor and deflated because he had failed the scare test. It reminds me of the Charlie Chaplin sequence in *Gold Rush* when the Tramp is celebrating Virginia's acceptance of his dinner invitation. He could have just exclaimed, "Yes!" or something, but instead, he jumps up on the bed, swings from the rafters, kicks pillow feathers all over the room.

Chapter 3: "Mr. Waternoose"

Mister Waternoose enters and establishes a basic premise of the movie: Monsters are more afraid of human children than the children are afraid of them. "Nothing is more toxic than a human child," explains Waternoose. One of the student monsters loses it right there and starts screaming about how he won't go into the room with a child. Waternoose explains why it is necessary to go in there. We have to do it in order to collect the screams of children in order to power Monstropolis. **This is a very smart piece of writing because it establishes that every time a monster enters a child's room, he has conflict with the situation. Remember, every scene needs conflict—conflict with self, with the situation, or with another character.**

Chapter 4: "Morning Workout"

Sulley and Mike are introduced. In the audio narration, director Pete Docter says that John Goodman (voice of Sulley) and Billy

Crystal (voice of Mike) did much of their recording while in the studio together. This is a departure from the way most voices are recorded for animated films, and I think it made a very big difference to the energy of this movie. Speaking from my background as an actor, I can assure you that acting alone is far more difficult than acting with a partner. **Acting is reacting.** If the other actor isn't there, you either have to depend on something that was recorded earlier or on your imagination.

The morning workout routine establishes how hard Sulley works to be good at his job of scaring children. The relationship between Sulley and Mike is not really clear yet, but we presume they are friends just based on the fact that Mike is in Sulley's bedroom in the morning.

In terms of scene construction, **Sulley has conflict with his situation because he would probably prefer to sleep in.** Mike also has conflict with Sulley's preference for sleeping. It is all resolved as Sulley gets enthusiastically into the exercising. By the end of the scene, there is no conflict, which is okay. It is resolved.

When the Monsters, Inc. commercial comes on television, Mike immediately runs to watch himself on TV. The acting note here is that you should **play an action until something happens to make you play a different action.** The commercial is the thing that happens to cause Mike to do something else. The transition is seamless, as it should be. It is motivated by emotion, as it should be. And it exposes more information about Mike's character, namely that he is something of a ham.

I like Mike's reaction to the fact that his face on TV was covered by the Monsters, Inc. logo. We see him think it through. **Always try to animate thoughts.** The thought process seems to be, "How do I feel about this? Am I disappointed? No, heck, at least I was on TV!" And he celebrates. There is a very fundamental principle of empathy at work here. **We empathize with** emotion, and we are attracted to the survival mechanism. If Mike had gone into a funk when he saw his face covered by the logo, we would have felt sorry for him, but we would not have felt as much empathy. That single moment was very important in the introduction of this character. It shows emotional range, internal negotiation. Very nice.

Chapter 5: "Monstropolis"

This is what I call a connective scene. Not much conflict, but it exposes some information and gets the characters from one place to another. **Every movie has connective scenes. You just can't overuse them. Audiences are looking for conflict, negotiation, and resolution.**

Note that when Sulley and Mike leave their apartment and head for work, a family of birds is in the background. The female bird tells her husband to have a good day, he assures her he will, and then he flies off into the sky. The scene goes by so fast that you might miss it if you aren't looking for it, but it is a marvelous bit. It establishes the kinds of people/creatures that live in Monstropolis and, of course, a work-bound bird would fly, not walk.

Newspaper in stand: "Rolling Blackout—Scream Shortage." Children are increasingly hard to scare in modern times. This helps establish conflict. A Pixar animator told me once that, in that studio, they have a policy of always trying to "sand the underside of the drawer." That is an excellent policy for storytelling. Audiences are very smart and they pick up more tiny details on-screen than you might think they would.

Chapter 6: "Monsters, Inc."

This is mostly connective, too. Mike's relationship with Celia is established, and the Pixar team stuck in an homage to stop-motion legend Ray Harryhausen. We are starting now to see that Mike is wound up like a top 100 percent of the time. Note his internal rhythm. **Every character has a rhythm.**

The movement of Mike and Sulley is purposeful because they are both heading for the Monsters Floor. They're going to work. **The purpose of movement is destination.**

Chapter 7: "Randall"

We return to scenes with conflict. Mike has conflict with the situation when he can't get his locker door to stay closed. Then Randall appears and, immediately, the conflict shifts from conflict with situation to conflict with another character. Once again, the transition is seamless.

Randall is a bully, and the storytellers have used this character trait effectively in this sequence. They needed to establish that Sulley is in head-to-head competition with Randall, but they still needed to have a justification for Randall turning up in the locker room. Evidently, he was motivated to come to the locker room by the prospect of intimidating Mike and bumping chests with Sulley. Remember, **your characters need to have a reason for entering a scene plus a reason for exiting.**

Chapter 8: "The Scare Floor"

This sequence works on several levels at once. We get our first look at the actual mechanics of the scare procedures, more characters are introduced, and further conflict is established. There is conflict with the situation for every character we see. Yes, they are in conflict with one another in that there is a competition, but this is not a conflict between characters because there is not a clear negotiation. Sulley is in conflict with Randall, but it is indirect, through the numerical scoreboard. In an acting sense, his conflict is with his situation. He is negotiating to hit ever higher scare numbers. As he accomplishes that, he simultaneously wins against Randall. It is very clever writing and scene construction. Much information is being exposed via well-constructed negotiations that are being played out in the present moment.

Observe that the movie has so far not used a single moment of flashback. And look at how much information they have conveyed in these first eight chapters. It is quite an impressive accomplishment.

Chapter 9: "23–19"

The purpose of this scene is to establish one more time how toxic human children are to the monsters. George gets a child's sock on his back and has to be decontaminated. The Child Detection Agency (CDA) springs into action. The acting principle is that you **play an action until something happens to make you play a different one.** George emerges from the child's room feeling very good about his scare numbers for the day. The sock on his back is the thing that happens to cause him to play a different action. So, too, does the sock cause everybody on the Scare Floor to play a different action. The CDA arrives, full of motivation to enter the scene. **This sequence is an adrenaline moment for George. He will never forget the day he got the sock stuck on his back.**

Once the sock is destroyed and George is decontaminated, Mr. Waternoose settles down with a cup of sludge as he bemoans the difficulty of running the family business. **Conflict with situation.**

Chapter 10: "End of the Day"

Mike: "The love boat is about to set sail . . . I tell ya, buddy, that face of hers makes my heart go—Yikes!!" **This is a good example of playing an action until something happens to make**

you play a different one. Roz appears unexpectedly, motivating Mike's extreme reaction. **It also is a good example of the principle that acting is both doing and reacting.** To break it down even further, into a thought process, Mike is thinking about Celia when Roz appears. The thought process is: "What's this? Ohmigod, it's Roz!" This leads to the physical action in which he cowers and protects himself with his arms. That is a defensive gesture wholly motivated by fear. Then when he adjusts to Roz being there, he knows she won't hurt him and so he relaxes his body a bit. **The more specific the acting choices, the better it will play.**

Roz's entrance gives Mike conflict with the situation. Her exit is followed by Celia's entrance, which further extends conflict with the situation. When Sulley offers to file Mike's paperwork for him, that resolves the negotiation. Mike exits to go to dinner with Celia.

Chapter 11: "Boo!"

The thing I like most about this chapter is that it closely follows Sulley's thought process. **Note how specific his thoughts are when he first discovers the door on the Scare Floor after hours.** The thought process goes this way: "What is that, a door? Yes, it is a door." Then he looks left and right to see if maybe someone is working late. "No, nobody here." He approaches the door and looks at the control panel. "Somebody must have forgotten to send the door back up after they got off work." Then he looks up and sees the bright red light on the door. "No, the door is ready for a scare monster to enter. This is weird." He opens the door and peers inside, thinking he will see a scare monster in there. "No, the room is quiet, and the kid must be sleeping." He backs out of the room and closes the door. He looks again at the red light over the door. "It must be broken." He taps the light to see if it maybe has a short in it. He hears the thump-thump sound. He looks to the left and the right, searching for where that sound is coming from. "No, it isn't to the left or right." Thump. He looks down at the floor. A human child! Transition! Acting rule: **Play an action until something happens to make you play a different action. As I counted them, there are at least seventeen specific thoughts in a forty-five-second sequence, beginning with Sulley's discovery of the door and ending with his reaction to Boo.**

The remainder of the chapter proceeds action to action to action as Sulley tries to get rid of the kid and the evidence. Extreme conflict with the situation. **This is also an adrenaline moment for Sulley.** When he turns eighty-five and looks back on his life, he will always remember the day he met Boo.

Chapter 12: "Harryhausen's"

Celia and Mike flirt with one another in the restaurant. **Lovers are very reactive to one another. Note the eye contact and body language.**

When Sulley turns up outside the window at an inopportune moment, it shifts the action into another transition. Mike has been playing an action (courting Celia) in pursuit of an objective (something romantic after dinner, perhaps?) while overcoming an obstacle (his own lack of grace). Sulley's face in the window introduces a whole new form of conflict.

When Boo gets out of the carrying case inside the restaurant, all hell breaks loose. Study how specific are the reactions of the background characters. You have a room full of them, and each has a unique life and a value system.

Also, notice the background characters when the interviews are happening on the street. "I tried to run from it, but it picked me up with its mind powers and shook me like a dog." Just like in real life, locals are fascinated by the presence of a camera and are waving and grinning, hoping to see themselves on the evening news. That is a well-observed moment. **Shakespeare says that actors should hold the mirror up to nature.** A scene can be brought to life with compelling background performances.

Chapter 13: "Back of the Apartment"

Sulley and Mike go from acting-moment to acting-moment trying to calm down Boo so they can have a second just to consider how to proceed from here. The obstacle is that a two-year-old child is unpredictable.

Observe that Boo is not often pushed to behave in ways that would not be credible for a two-year-old. We in the audience recognize that because we have all been around little kids at one time or another.

Chapter 14: "Bedtime"

Minor quibble: At the top of this sequence, Mike is still over the top. He is yelling about how Boo is a killing machine, and he is still calling her "it" instead of "she." This feels a bit pushed to me. I think Mike would be smart enough to figure out that if he yells like that, he is going to upset the kid and maybe make her start crying again. It feels to me like he would be walking on eggshells instead of charging like a bull.

This is a transitional scene because first Sulley and then Mike have to start coming to terms with the reality that Boo is nonthreatening. They have been conditioned to be afraid of human children. After this scene, Sulley and Mike will both be on the same page in their efforts to return Boo to her home.

Chapter 15: "Sneaking Boo to Work"

As Mike and Sulley enter the main Monsters, Inc. building at the top of the chapter, they expect to encounter a relatively normal working environment. They do not know that the CDA teams are swarming over the place. When they see all those orange suits, they react. **The acting principle here is that you act on expectation.** In other words, Mike and Sulley have every reason to expect that, inside the front doors of the company, they will see a certain kind of behavior and environment. When they discover that the reality is different from that, then they react and shift gears. In life, we always act on expectation. You are, at this very moment, expecting that I will finish up this thought and then get on to the next acting point, and so you are reading along accordingly. If I START SCREAMING AT YOU AND TELLING YOU THAT A TARANTULA IS ON YOUR SHOULDER, YOU WILL BE SURPRISED!!! Heh.

Chapter 16: "Potty Break"

Bathroom hide-and-seek. There is not a lot of conflict in this scene, but it is fun anyway and it establishes that Sulley has actually begun to enjoy Boo's presence. **Emotion tends to lead to action.**

Chapter 17: "Randall's Plot"

Mike discovers Sulley playing hide-and-seek with Boo. Sulley refers to Boo as "she," Mike is still referring to her as "it." I think it is time for Mike to get off the "it" thing. This is a script issue, not an animation issue. The animation is swell. All of the movement is motivated by emotion, and the characters have clear motivations for entering the scene.

Did Randall go to the bathroom before he washed his hands?

The sequence in which Randall knocks open the stall doors is excellent. The force with which the doors open show that Randall is very strong and could do damage to you if he got hold of you. It also makes him quite animal-like. That staccato movement from one stall door to another is very much like lizards move in the wild. They scoot a short distance and stop very still. Then they scoot and stop again. Humans don't move like that.

In terms of scene construction, all of the characters have conflict with the situation.

Chapter 18: "The Wrong Door"

Mike discovers that Sulley has named the kid Boo. "If you name it, you will get attached to it!" he protests. This explains why Mike continues to refer to Boo as "it," but I really think this was not necessary. I can't see how the plot would have been hurt if Mike was allowed earlier to recognize the gender of the child. If Randall can see it, why can't Mike? It would have made Mike a bit more accessible if he warmed to Boo earlier.

The kissing sequence in the hall between Mike and Celia is cute and motivated. When Mike drops Celia and runs for his life, I would have liked to see Celia swoon a bit. Mike is a big take-charge kisser, after all. Instead, she was left sort of muttering.

Chapter 19: "Mike on the Run"

Mike tries to find a place to hide from Randall. Running is the action, and escaping Randall is the objective. The obstacle is that Randall is faster than Mike and can be invisible.

The transaction between Randall and Mike in the hallway is basically a status negotiation. Randall is a bully. Mike acknowledges the strength and dominance of the bigger character. Notice how physically close Randall gets to Mike? **Each of us has a space bubble around us, an area of personal space into which we only allow family and intimates. We get uncomfortable when a stranger gets into our space.** We in the audience empathize with the feeling of being intruded upon that way.

Chapter 20: "The Trash Compactor"

There is an old rule of comedy that says you can't repeat the same gag more than three times. When Sulley is watching the trash compacting machine, he faints four times. The fourth one doesn't work. When he sees the final block of compacted metal, supposedly containing the remains of Boo, it would have worked better if he had approached it, maybe put his hands on it, and then sagged forward onto it. To have him faint again and fall over backward doesn't work, especially because in the next sequence, we see him sadly carrying the cube of metal.

Chapter 21: "Mike Kidnapped"

There is a nice transitional moment when Sulley changes tactics and decides to go after Randall. Sulley is under the worktable, holding Boo. Randall is invisibly lurking. After Randall leaves, there is a microsecond transition that you can see if you slow down the replay. You can see Sulley think "Enough is enough," shift his body into an attack gear, and start chasing Randall. The motivating emotion is anger. Sulley has been pushed around enough. He is not going to be afraid of Randall any longer.

Chapter 22: "The Scream Machine"

This is a well-constructed scene. If we didn't know before that Randall is a full-tilt villain, we do now. A villain can be defined as a regular person with a fatal flaw. Randall's fatal flaw is ambition. This scene shows the extreme lengths he will go to in order to achieve power over others. It took a lot of effort to build the Scream Extractor!

Randall's objective is to knock off the competition and emerge at the top of a new Monsters, Inc. power structure. The action he is playing is to test out the Scream Extractor. If Boo had been in the box as he thought she was, he would be well along his way. Instead, Mike was in there, so Randall has to try a new course of action.

Randall has undergone a transformation and is determined to save Mike and stop Randall. He is taking calculated risks as he unplugs the Scream Extractor and then frees Mike.

An awful lot of information is being exposed in this chapter, and it is 100 percent justified by the ongoing action in the story. It is a pretty perfect sequence, and it works emotionally. By now, we in the audience are rooting like crazy for Mike and Randall and Boo.

Chapter 23: "Sulley Scares Boo"

I very much like the moment in which Mr. Waternoose says, "It is all about presence, about how you enter the room!" And at that very moment, Sulley, Mike, and Boo enter the room. The force with which Sulley knocks open the door is significant. He is physically powerful and is on a mission. He enters with authority and determination.

The sequence leading up to Sulley's magnificent roar involves wonderful acting. Sulley is trying his best to make his point with Mr, Waternoose, but Waternoose is playing a status transaction. Finally, out of exasperation with Waternoose, Sulley lets loose with the mother of all roars. My sense is that he is actually roaring at Waternoose! He is roaring at the awful situation he is in with Boo. Lovely acting. Play this sequence slowly a couple of times. Watch the thoughts and transitions.

When Mr. Waternoose sees Boo, he exclaims, "A child!" Mike steps in and reassures him, "Sir, she's not toxic. . . ." At last! Mike is referring to Boo by her gender instead of as an "it." I only wish we in the audience had been allowed to see that character transition. It happened off camera.

The Sulley and Boo scene that comes toward the end of the chapter is marvelous. Sulley has to come face to face (via TV replay of the previous simulated scare sequence) with the reality of what his life has become. He is a person who scares little kids for a living. Watch how his expression changes like currents in the ocean as this slowly occurs to him. I particularly like the very slight twitch in his right eye's lower lid. It is extremely subtle but signifies a moment of truth. **Moments of truth and insight tend to be very still.** Time seems to stop.

Chapter 24: "Banished"

Mike and Sulley have a magnificent scene in which they both come to terms with basic values in life. Most of it is nonverbal. **Acting has almost nothing to do with words.** Play this sequence a couple of times and watch the back-and-forth between them. It is all in the eyes.

Sulley makes the decision to go save Boo even though that means leaving Mike and maybe freezing to death on the way. He is a changed character from the one we met at the beginning of the movie. He is more mature, more knowing, and has turned into a hero. This is excellent storytelling.

Chapter 25: "Sulley Rescues Boo"

We learn that Mr. Waternoose has been in cahoots with Randall all along. His motivation is monetary, to "save the company."

I like the way that Sulley pulls the door off the secret tunnel to the Scream Extractor. For the first time in the movie, he is using his incredible strength purely for good. He is going to rescue Boo. If you play that sequence slowly, you will see that his left arm trembles with the strain of breaking the door from its hinges. That, too, is excellent performance because it establishes the degree of commitment Sulley has.

Chapter 26: "Schmoopsie Poo!"

The important transition in this scene belongs to Celia. Talk about connecting the dots! When she sees Boo, she realizes in a flash that Mike is telling her the truth about the conspiracy. She hears Randall chasing up the hallway and immediately chooses to help thwart him.

Chapter 27: "The Door Vault"

This is plain old-fashioned Hitchcockian storytelling and it is delightful. All that action on the roller-coaster world of doors is breathtaking. I love the way they have Sulley, Mike, and Randall chase in and out of various countries. And the payoff is good, even if it is a bit of a stretch to believe that Boo could be mature enough to jump on Randall's back at the very last moment. That kind of thinking isn't typical of a two-year-old, even one that is no longer afraid of monsters. But it's a small point, really. By this time, we in the audience are looking for resolution. It is time for the movie to be over and so we don't look too carefully at whether or not Boo's behavior is logically appropriate. If it had happened earlier in the movie, we would have.

Chapter 28: "Tricking Waternoose"

Sulley and Mike set up Waternoose to expose himself as a traitor to Monstropolis. Waternoose evidently has no compunction about bringing real children into the city, just as long as it saves the company's bottom line. He is captured and taken off by the CDA.

CDA Number One turns out to be Roz the bookkeeper. I like the way her entrance establishes a certain humanity in her. Up until now, she has just been a shrew, a bully to Mike. Now we see that she has a tender core. Her instructions regarding Boo are actually quite humane and appropriate. Sulley should send her back home but, after he does so, her door is to be shredded so that she is never seen again.

Sulley's reaction to the news that he will never see Boo again is good acting. Watch his body sag.

Chapter 29: "Good-bye"

More excellent performance. Sulley is very reactive to the moment once he is in Boo's bedroom. He is stalling, not wanting to go back to Monstropolis. He plays with her and, finally, realizes that the time has come. In the audio narration to the movie, Pete Docter mentions how they tried to make Sulley's eyes just a little misty in this sequence. That is a very wise choice. Full tears would have been too much. Sulley would not want Boo to see him cry. This is a good reflection of how people behave in real life. **We do not easily share our emotions with one another.** Shakespeare again: hold the mirror up to nature.

Chapter 30: "The Laugh Floor"

A child's laugh can be more powerful than a child's scream. What a lovely idea! What an excellent payoff for the story.

Chapter 31: "Kitty"

Mike is all heart, as it turns out. It took a lot of effort to reconstruct Boo's bedroom door, but he did it out of love. Sulley is appropriately touched by the gesture.

It is perfect that we do not see Boo again at the end of the movie. We see her only as she is reflected in Sulley's face and in his emotional reaction to her. **Sometimes when you are telling a good story, you have to know when to stop.**

Chapter 32: End Credits

6. Grave of the Fireflies

Studio Ghibli (1988, original Japanese version; 1998, English version)

Producer: Tohru Hara

Director: Isao Takahata

Screenwriter: Isao Takahata

Based on the novel by Akiyuki Nosaka

Editor: Takeshi Seyama

Art Director: Nizou Yamamoto

Animators: Hideaki Anno, Yoshiyuki Hane, Kuniyuki Ishii, Sodatsu Ishikuro, Megumi Kagawa, Hideo Kawauchi, Masuji Kigami, Yoshifumi Kondo, Noriko Moritomo, Hiroshi Ogawa, Toshiyasu Okada, Reiko Okuyama, Shunji Saida, Akio Sakai, Michiyo Sakurai, Noboru Takano, Kitarou Takasaka, Yasuomi Umetsu, Shôjurô Yamauchi, Atsuko Ôtani, Noriko Ôzeki

Voice Cast: Tsutomu Tatsumi (Seita), Ayano Shiraishi (Setsuko), Yoshiko Shinohara (Mother), Akemi Yamaguchi (Aunt), Rhoda Chrosite (Setsuko, English-language version), Crispin Freeman (Doctors, Old Man, English-language version), Dan Green (additional voices, English version), Amy Jones (Aunt, English-language version), George Leaver (additional voices, English-language version), J. Robert Spencer (Seita, English-language version), Nick Sullivan (additional voices, English-language version), Veronica Taylor (Mother, English-language version)

Overview

Seita and his four-year-old sister are orphaned in the WWII Allied attacks on Kobe, Japan. This is the story of their ultimately futile attempts to survive. As Roger Ebert said in his *Chicago Sun-Times* review, "This is one of the greatest anti-war movies ever made. It just happens to be animation." **This kind of plot line automatically sets the main characters into conflict with their situation.** Even connective scenes will have conflict. Conflict is an essential element of drama and so, from a storytelling perspective, this movie begins with runners already on first and second base. Music is also used very effectively in *Grave of the Fireflies* to establish mood.

Analysis

Chapter 1: "Opening"

The story begins with its resolution. The spirit of Seita, a deceased fourteen-year-old Japanese boy, faces the camera. He is dressed in what appears to be neat military garb, and he has a haunted expression on his face. He looks into the camera and says simply: "September 21, 1945. That was the night I died." The camera pans away from him and moves into a dingy, mostly deserted Japanese train station. We discover the real-life fourteen-year-old Seita at the moment of his death, sitting collapsed against a pillar. He is emaciated, he has sores on his body, and his clothes are in tatters. The camera begins with his shoeless feet and moves slowly up his body until we see that his breathing is shallow and that he is near death. **In movies, the audience will figure everything**

shown on screen means something, and they will continually be trying to make sense of it. The opening sequence of this movie is very powerful visually and requires the audience to start right out by working hard. We see that the boy in uniform is the same one who leans against the column; we see that, in death, he is restored to physical health; we see that, even in death, he appears tormented and tortured, and we see that he must have gone through seven stages of hell in order to get into the awful condition at the time of his death. **I like the way the camera begins with a study of the boy's bare feet. Bare feet tell a story all by themselves. By the time a boy is shoeless in the middle of a city, his situation would be dire indeed.** This is wonderful storytelling. Only forty seconds have elapsed since the movie began and, so far, there has been only that single line, "September 21, 1945. That was the night I died." Already, a powerful mood has been established.

It is an interesting storytelling device to disclose the ending of the story at the beginning. Because the audience knows how it ends, every scene in the movie will be measured against what they already know will be the ultimate outcome. Many playwrights and novelists have successfully used this device. Harold Pinter's play *Betrayal,* for instance, has such a structure and is one of my favorites.

A person on the train station cleaning crew discovers Seita's lifeless body and searches through his pockets, looking for identification. He finds only a rusted candy tin that appears to be rubbish. No candy in it, only a white powder. He does not realize that the powder is actually the cremated remains of Seita's four-year-old sister, Setsuko.

When the worker tosses the can into some bushes outside the station, the lid comes off and some of the ashes spill onto the ground. Setsuko's spirit magically arises into the night, just like so many lovely fireflies, and she is soon joined by the spirit Seita. They begin a journey back through their lives. From this point on, *Grave of the Fireflies* will move back and forth between the afterlife perspective and the present-moment perspective. **The amazing thing about this opening chapter is how much information the director and animators conveyed without words. It is extraordinarily effective filmmaking.**

Chapter 2: "Air Raid"

In this series of sequences, we see firsthand the horrors of a massive napalm bomb attack on a city. **All of the characters have conflict with the situation.** The air attacks amount to a huge **adrenaline moment for all of the characters.** If they survive the attack, they win; if they die, they lose. As it evolves, Seita and Setsuko's mother is killed in these attacks. She loses, but her children live and survive for the time being. The tension in the chapter builds as the American B-47 aircraft get ever closer and then begin dropping bombs. Because the napalm bombs are delayed-reaction devices, there is an unexpected escalation in tension/conflict even after the bombs hit the ground and buildings. We think we have seen the worst of it, and then the bombs turn into explosive fiery infernos. Note that when Seita emerges from his home after the first bombardment, he erroneously concludes that the worst is over and that he has survived. His gait suggests that he believes the conflict has been resolved. But then the bombs start fires, and Seita is terrified. **Emotion tends to lead to action.** Note that his pace quickens considerably. Seita carries his frightened sister to a dried-up canal and hides among some bunkers. The child is clearly terrified and clings trembling to her brother's arm.

Chapter 3: "We're Safe Here"

The first images in this chapter are of dead soldiers, terrified and huddled citizens, uncontrolled fire, and even one man commiting hari-kari. **I think part of the reason these images are so** powerful and emotionally compelling is precisely because they are animated. Animation is not real; war is. We in the audience are being forced to separate the two. It is a lesson in life; it is shamanistic storytelling. I very much like the way the animators are making the audience do so much work.

As the city burns, we cut to the sweetness and innocence of Setsuko, a young child. She is comforted and delighted with her small purse that is filled with colorful buttons. Seita is charmed and tells her that she is indeed rich, which delights her. Note that her laugh is genuine. Children this age are incapable of playing social games. If they are sad, they cry; if they are happy, they laugh. Even with a horrible war within easy earshot, this fact of life is true. The sequence is important because it helps establish just how much we lose when a child dies. The world is that much less innocent. It also helps further display the values of Seita. It is clear that he will protect his sister with his own life.

Seita and Setsuko walk into the devastated city that was their home. They search for their mother. Seita develops an irritation in her eye from the napalm fumes. Their situation becomes even more dire, and we easily empathize.

Chapter 4: "My Mother"

This chapter contains one of the most extraordinary and powerful sequences in the entire movie. It literally takes my breath away, and I want to speak about it at some length.

The sequence happens at the playground area after Seita has given Setsuko their mother's ring for safekeeping. The child is disconsolate and wants to see her mom. Seita cannot comfort her this time, and so he leaves her crouching and alone and sobbing, and he walks a short distance away to the playground pull-up bar. There is a very long hold on this tableau, the child crying in the foreground and Seita sitting slumped with his back to us in the background. Then, suddenly, Seita springs up, telling his sister to watch him because this is something he does very well. He leaps up and grabs the pull-up bar and begins to do flip after flip after flip. This is the point at which I lost my breath.

We humans act to survive. Seita's situation is dire. His mother is dying, his father is somewhere at sea fighting a battle, their home is burned to the ground, and the city is in ashes. He is only fourteen years old and has to care for his sister, who is every inch a child that needs her mom. He is feeling impotent, powerless. It requires an act of almost heroic willpower to leap onto the pull-up bar. With that action, he reduces the terrible world to one that he can briefly control and even master. We in the audience empathize with his fear and determination. We can feel his strength. **The acrobatics on the bar become metaphoric. No! I will not die!** Awesome filmmaking. **Animators are shamans. You draw a circle in the dirt, and the tribe gathers. They are looking for lessons in life. The roots of theatre are in stories of survival. The human spirit is on powerful display in this sequence.**

Returning now to the top of the chapter, Seita sees his mother, who is obviously suffering from fatal wounds. This would be an **adrenaline moment** for him. Despite the obvious, he hopes against hope that she will survive. There are several important acting notes to consider. A bespectacled man, presumably a doctor or medical volunteer, gives Seita his mother's ring, which has been cut from her finger. As Seita handles the ring, he feels close to his mother, and we empathize. In acting, **this is known as a "sense memory."** The ring will reappear throughout the story, each time delivering an emotional punch. Next, note that after Seita sees his bandaged and bleeding mother, **two subsequent shots involve very long holds. This stillness is a strong device in Japanese animation.** In the first, Seita stares at the distant devastation and still burning fires. Then we have a medium-close shot of his face.

Despite the fact that there is zero movement in the animation, **we empathize with Seita's pain.** We see him coming to terms with how dire his situation really is. We get a glimpse into the emotional journey of a boy who will too soon become a man.

Later, Seita and Setsuko move into the home of their aunt. Seita leaves his sister there for the moment and visits the hospital where his mother was taken. There his worst fear comes true as he learns that she has died. He attends her cremation and carries her ashes home in a small wooden box.

Chapter 5: "Welcome Back"

Seita hides the box containing his mother's ashes in the bushes outside his aunt's house. This is an indication that **he has conflict with himself as well as conflict with the situation.** How and when should he tell Setsuko that their mother is dead? Now? Later? Yes, now; no, later. . . .

Setsuko hears the front door open and runs excitedly and expectantly into the foyer to see her mother. Emotion leads to action. Setsuko's entrance reflects happy expectation. When Seita lies and tells Setsuko that their mom is still sick, he does so with his back to the child. Acting-wise, that is right. His face would betray the lie. Setsuko returns to her room where she takes her mom's ring from her purse and holds it. Again, **we empathize with the emotion of sense memory.**

The next day Seita returns to the burned-out remains of his former home and digs up supplies he had buried prior to the air raids. There is a vat containing dried fish, butter, eggs, and a tin of fruit candy. This is the same tin we saw in the first sequence of the movie. It will later contain the ashes of Setsuko and so has instant emotional impact on the audience.

As Seita heads back to his aunt's house with the supplies, he comes across a broken water main and pauses to bathe. It is a simple pleasure that happens amidst the ruins of the city. **It is another act of survival and carries with it more emotion than would a simple bath in another context.**

Chapter 6: "She's Dead?"

The primary purpose of this chapter is to establish that Seita and Setsuko are increasingly isolated. When Seita tells his aunt that his mother is in fact dead, she does not try at all to comfort him. This would be a moment of tender vulnerability for the boy, and we empathize with his fear and sadness. We know how it feels to want to be held. The boy is no doubt tired of having to be strong and could do with a good cry and a soft shoulder. The aunt's true color is selfishness. The instant after she gasps with surprise, "She's dead?", the aunt reprimands Seita for having hidden the bad news. **The acting lesson here is in how quickly the aunt evidently changes her colors. A person does not fundamentally change from generous to selfish in a moment. The fact that her behavior shifts so dramatically and so fast shows that selfishness and coldness is her true self. It has been there all along, and the warm hospitality we have been seeing was a façade. You could read even more into the transformation, in fact. Her turn mirrors the betrayal of the simple world Seita and Setsuko occupied before the bombs dropped. Nothing is what it appears to be.**

As was the case in Chapter 3, we now have sequences that emphasize the innocence in Setsuko. The first is when Seita takes a bath with her and catches bubbles in the washcloth. It is such a simple, childlike pleasure! And later when they go into the night and catch fireflies. In story structure, it is significant that capturing fireflies happens now rather than earlier. We can sense that the aunt is ultimately going to turn against them. **Fireflies have a bright and short life. The same fate awaits Seita and Setsuko.**

Chapter 7: "Not Again"

We all can relate to hunger. It is basic, a primal drive. We must eat in order to live. This sequences of this chapter show that Seita and Setsuko are not getting proper nutrition. The child is developing rashes. We also learn that Seita's former workplace was bombed and so he has no place to work; and his school burned down. He has no place to go. He is dependent on his aunt, and she is giving preferential treatment at the dinner table to her male boarder, her daughter—and to herself. It is increasingly clear that his aunt does not want him and Setsuko to be permanent houseguests. Note that she carefully gives Seita and Setsuko broth only, while giving her daughter and the boarder rice. The food she is dispensing is, of course, the same that Seita brought to the aunt in Chapter 5.

Chapter 8: "The Beach"

Seita takes Setsuko to the beach. They run and play. Increasingly, they can find relief only in the simplest things. Hunger is a constant companion, and the child is getting sicker. The accompanying music to their beach romp is bright and light. The beach itself has no signs of war. They play and there is no overt conflict except that Setsuko has a pronounced rash on her back.

Exhausted from play, they collapse on the beach and Setsuko plays with a crab. She follows it until she comes across a dead man under a mat. The reality of their situation again chases away the few pleasures they can find. Seita pulls her away from the corpse and they go for another swim. In the water, Seita has a fantasy of life as it used to be when their mother was alive and there was plenty to eat. Then air-raid sirens break the pleasant fantasy, bringing him back to brutal reality. We see another approaching formation of B-47s on the horizon. **The conflict in the beach scenes is with the situation. Remember, the element** of conflict/obstacle is necessary for strong storytelling. As I mentioned at the beginning of these notes, *Grave of the Fireflies* has built-in conflict from start to finish because it involves these two people trying to survive in an inhospitable environment. So, yes, the playing on the beach is fun and seemingly untroubled, but it only works emotionally because of the underlying conflict/obstacle.

Chapter 9: "They're Mama's!"

The most compelling acting lesson in this chapter is the way that Setsuko struggles to protect her mom's kimonos. The aunt wants to trade them for rice, but the robes are one of the remaining few emotional links Setsuko has to her mother. Note how far the animators went with the sequence. The child literally tries to wrestle the kimonos out of her aunt's grasp. In such a structured society, it would be remarkable for a child to confront an adult this way. The fact that she does so lets us see the depth of the child's desire to survive. **Her grasp on her aunt's arm is almost primal.**

Later at dinner, aunt serves up some of the rice that came from the kimono trade. Again, she shortchanges Seita and Setsuko in favor of her daughter and border. When Seita objects that "it is our rice," the aunt turns even more ugly, ordering them to henceforth make their own dinners. She tells them they are ungrateful and suggests they go live with relatives in Tokyo. Seita would happily do that if only he knew how to contact those distant relatives. He and his sister are being pushed out of what amounts to a temporary nest.

Chapter 10: "7,000 Yen"

Seita and Setsuko visit the bank to see how much money their mom had in her account. While Seita is inside the bank, Setsuko observes a loving and happy mother-daughter scene on the sidewalk. It makes her feel sadder and more isolated. **Notice Setsuko's power center in this sequence. She crouches, shrinking ever smaller. Like a firefly, her light is getting dimmer.** Seita comes out of the bank and, when she complains of hunger and thirst, he offers her another fruit drop. This time she does not squeal with glee at the prospect. Fruit drops no longer satisfy. Later, Seita uses money from the account to purchase a stove, some food, a comb for Setsuko, and an umbrella. Again, we have a sequence of childlike happiness when they walk home with the rain beating on the umbrella. **Emotion tends to lead to action. They sing a child's song.** Simple pleasures are getting fewer, but they still work.

Seita cooks dinner for Setsuko and himself. They stuff their tummies and then lounge. Note that when Seita kicks back on the mat and sighs with pleasure at his satisfied appetite, young Setsuko anxiously continues to eat. **Her eating has shifted from a pleasurable thing to something essential for survival. There is a determined and primal quality to it.**

Chapter 11: "Rice for Two"

Their circumstances worsen when Setsuko goes for his rice ration. There is not nearly enough to sustain him and Setsuko until the next ration in July. Still, Seita acts to protect Setsuko's innocence and happiness. On the way back home he gives her the last of the fruit drops. **Acting note: There is a small negotiation (conflict with situation) in this brief sequence. Setsuko's cry is a negotiating ploy.** A child cries when she wants or needs something. In this case, it works because Seita finds a couple of remaining fruit drops that are stuck to the inside of the can. He shakes them into her hand. **She wins the negotiation.**

Later at home, they fill the empty fruit drop tin with water, swish it around and enjoy a little tea party. One more simple pleasure. Significantly, however, the fruit drops are now gone. That pleasure at least will no longer be available.

Chapter 12: "So Selfish"

Setsuko has nightmares and screams for her mother. The aunt comes into the room and reprimands her for the noise, which is keeping her daughter and boarder awake. She tells them they are nothing but pests and trouble. Seita puts Setsuko on his back and walks into the firefly-filled night, trying to calm her back to sleep. Suddenly, we hear another air-raid siren. **Note the long shot of them running and hunting for a place to hide. At one point, they are precisely the same size as the fireflies.** They and the fireflies are siblings in a way.

After the aunt scolds them for playing the piano when "a war is going on," Seita has a good idea: he and Setsuko will go live in a bomb shelter. **Note the shift in their energy. There is a spring in their step. The reason this works is because they have found something they can do to survive. They are feeling empowered.** They return to their burned-out former home and retrieve as many belongings from the rubble as they can, load everything on a cart, and head for their new home in the shelter. As they disappear out of sight down the road, we hear Setsuko giggling with glee at the new adventure.

Chapter 13: "Let's Eat"

They prepare their new home and gather supplies. **Note once again the physicality of the child. When she is happy, she is very happy. She disguises nothing emotionally.** Also, did you notice that the first item Seita unpacks in their new cave home is the box containing their mother's ashes? That is excellent story development. The animators could have, by now, put that box aside. The fact that they carry it on through the movie adds to our experience of empathy with the two main characters.

They eat the last of their rice. At this point in the story, Setsuko and Seita begin to live off the land. They have no more access to store-bought food and so they plan to eat frogs and mollusks and wild herbs. We notice that both of them are now scratching rashes.

Chapter 14: "Fireflies"

Setsuko is afraid of the dark and so they collect a lot of fireflies and release them inside the mosquito netting of their bedroom. It is another moment of innocent pleasure, and it leads to Seita thinking of his father and a majestic naval review he watched some years earlier. It is a memory of happier days. Setsuko falls asleep. **Acting note: After Setsuko is asleep, Seita moves to hold her. She pushes him away. He turns his back on her and pulls himself into something close to a fetal position. Emotion tends to lead to action. He needs to be held.** Setsuko is not the one to be holding him, and so he holds himself.

Chapter 15: "So Young"

Setsuko is burying the fireflies that gave so much light and happiness the night before. She tells Seita that she knows their mother is dead and also in a grave because their aunt told her. At this point, Seita breaks down and cries. At last he can grieve. **Acting note: Even as he cries, he stands erect and facing Setsuko. He is strong and weak at the same time.** Setsuko breaks his heart further when she asks, "Why do fireflies have to die so soon?" The camera tracks to the inside of the shelter where two fireflies hover momentarily around their mom's box of ashes, and then their lights go out, leaving the cave in darkness. Another possible interpretation of the two fireflies is that they represent Setsuko and Seita. The fact that there are only two fireflies definitely caught my attention.

Chapter 16: "Ghost!"

A gang of boys happens by the shelter while Setsuko and Seita are away. They make fun of whoever lives there, tossing around the dried frogs and grated soybeans. The relevant story point is that, clearly, this kind of food is inadequate for survival. When the boys run away, I like it that one of them returns briefly to get the bucket. I realize this may seem on the surface to be insignificant, but all the animators really had to do was get the boys off screen. It required extra animation work to have him return to fetch his bucket. I believe that excellent storytelling is greatly enhanced by such attention to detail.

Then the scene shifts to Seita trying to purchase rice from a farmer. The farmer will not sell and will not share. Notice that both Seita and Setsuko are scratching their rashes continually. The symptoms of malnutrition are getting worse.

On their way back to the shelter, there is an air attack and they dive for cover in a vegetable garden. **When Seito sees the approaching jet and reacts, freeze-frame and watch the next few seconds slowly. Note his protective embrace of Setsuko. Note that when he dives for cover, he literally dives headfirst.** Hidden amid the vines, Seita discovers ripe tomatoes. Food! **People will act to survive, even if they must steal.**

Chapter 17: "My Sister's Sick"

This chapter is gut wrenching because it is so primal. We are literally reduced to focusing on bodily functions. Setsuko has diarrhea, another sign of malnutrition. Seita sneaks into a nearby vegetable garden to steal food for her and is caught by the farmer. Even as he is being beaten, he still tries to make away with the sugar cane. He does not simply flee. If he had fled, I suspect he could have outrun the farmer. But the conflict he has is not only with the farmer but with the fact that his sister is sick and needs food. He has to choose between his own survival and hers. In the end, he is beaten severely and taken to the police. After being released from police custody, he reunites with Setsuko. Acting note: When she runs to him and hugs his legs, Seita once again cries. **This time his tears are more a sign of misery and despair than of release.** He is hungry, bruised and battered, has a sick little sister, and is running out of options. **Note that Seita begins crying while standing. He is strong and weak at the same time. Then he crouches and embraces Setsuko and begins crying again. These are two related but distinct acting beats.**

Chapter 18: "Dinner"

Emotion tends to lead to action. Humans act to survive. Seita has resorted now to stealing from people's homes during air-raid alerts. Hunger and fear are driving him. Setsuko meanwhile is almost too weak to eat anything at all. She is fading fast now.

In the night, another air-raid alert sounds. Seita again robs from homes. On the way back to the cave/shelter, he pauses and laughs out loud. **Acting note: People rarely laugh out loud when they are alone. Seita's laugh is more manic than joyful. There is an edge to it.**

Chapter 19: "Doctor's Office"

Seita discovers Setsuko unconscious from hunger. He takes her to a doctor, who diagnoses her with malnutrition but offers no remedy. Seita reacts with anger. "Where do I get food?!" he demands. Outside the doctor's office he comes across a man cutting and delivering ice. He picks up an ice chip off the ground and feeds it to Setsuko. **Note the stillness in this sequence. The power is in what is not said.** Together, they fantasize about the wonderful foods they would most love to eat. Seita says he will withdraw the rest of their mom's money from the bank and buy food. Setsuko is beyond hunger and only wants to be held. He promises that after he gets her food this time, he will never leave her again. She smiles weakly. **Acting note: Even as the final bits of life ebb from her body she manages a smile. People act to survive. The last thing we do before we die is try to live. We in the audience empathize.**

Chapter 20: "Surrendered"

Seita goes to the bank and withdraws the final 3,000 yen. While in line, he overhears talk of Japan having surrendered. Then he learns that the entire naval fleet had been sunk. He flies into a violent panic, grabbing blindly at the man who delivered the news. "Is my father dead, too? Is that why he hasn't written?" **Acting note: Emotion tends to lead to action. The stakes are high and he loses control physically.** The man flings him to the ground. Sieta races from the bank and careens down the street. After he calms down, he takes from his pocket a much-handled photo of his father. He realizes now that both of his parents are dead. He dejectedly continues home to see Setsuko. **Note the shift in his power center. It is now much lower. His rhythm has slowed considerably.**

Chapter 21: "Rice Balls"

Setsuko is on her deathbed when Seita arrives. She is too weak to move and almost too weak to speak. She has rolled mud into pretend rice balls and generously offers them to him. He cries.

Seita cuts a slice of the watermelon he has brought for her and puts it to her lips. She murmurs that it is "good." He goes out the door to prepare more food for her. However, she dies then and there, while still holding the slice of watermelon. **Acting note: This scene has a lot of stillness in it. We are approaching the end of life. Nothing moves. Time stands still. Gravity is winning the negotiation.**

Chapter 22: "Lovely Day"

Seita lies on the bed and holds his lifeless sister in his arms. **Note how long the shots are held. One of them is fully ten seconds of zero movement.** Zero movement and yet the emotion and sense of loss that is conveyed is almost overwhelming. **Hayao Miyazaki explained in an interview once that this kind of stillness is called "ma." Stillness is good in animation if it is filled with emotion and intention.** Everything does not have to stay in constant motion. This is of course one of the distinguishing differences between Japanese-style animation and that of the West.

Then we have a fantasy sequence in which a happy Setsuko plays around the shelter door. She entertains herself with various games the same as any child with a normal life. She pricks her finger while mending a shirt and tastes the blood droplet that appears on her finger. We leave her like that, happy and at ease. The world is a less innocent place without her.

Chapter 23: "The Funeral"

Seita prepares his sister lovingly and then cremates her on a lovely hilltop. As the fire dies, so does the day. Fireflies spring to life and fill the sky. Seita, in voice-over, tells us that he never returned to the shelter he and Setsuko shared. We know from the first chapter where he went instead. And we know already how the story ends.

7. Toy Story 2

Pixar Animation Studios (1999)

Producers: Karen Robert Jackson, Helene Plotkin

Executive Producer: Sarah McArthur

Directors: Ash Brannon, Lee Unkrich, John Lasseter

Writers: John Lasseter, Peter Docter, Ash Brannon, Andrew Stanton, Rita Hsiao, Doug Chamberlain, Chris Webb

Animators: Nicolas Alan Barillaro, Stephen Barnes, Bobby Beck, Michael Berenstein, Ash Brannon, Jennifer Cha, Brett Coderre, Scott Clark, Melanie Cordan, David DeVan, Mark R. R. Farquhar, Ike Feldman, Andrew Gordon, Stephen Gregory, Jimmy Hayward, Timothy Hittle, Christina Yim, Kureha Yokoo, Nancy Kato, Adam Wood, James Ford Murphy, Peter Nash, Anthony Scott, Doug Sheppeck, Jeff Pratt, Karen Prell, Brett Pulliam, Bret "Brook" Parker, Michael Parks, Sanjay Patel, Ross Stevenson, Tim Crawfurd, Steven Clay Hunter, John Kahrs, Ethan Hurd, Karen Kiser, Bob Koch, Wendell Lee, Peter Lepeniotis, Shawn P. Krause, Dan Mason, Angus MacLane, Jon Mead, Billy Merritt, Karyn Metlen, Valerie Mih, Mark Oftedal, Bobby Podesta, Rich Quade, Mike Quinn, Roger Rose, Robert H. Russ, Gini Cruz Santos, Alan Sperling, Doug Sweetland, David Tart, J. Warren Trezevant, Mark A. Walsh, Tasha Wedeen, Kyle Balda (directing animator), Dylan Brown (directing animator), Glenn McQueen (directing animator)

Voice Cast: Tom Hanks (Sheriff Woody), Tim Allen (Buzz Lightyear of Star Command/Buzz Lightyear of Star Command II), Joan Cusack (Jessie the Yodeling Cowgirl), Kelsey Grammer (Stinky Pete the Prospector), Don Rickles (Mr. Potato Head), Jim Varney (Slinky Dog), Wallace Shawn (Rex the Green Dinosaur), John Ratzenberger (Hamm the Piggy Bank), Annie Potts (Bo Peep), Wayne Knight (Al "Chicken Man" McWhiggin the Toy Collector), John Morris (Andy Davis), Laurie Metcalf (Andy's Mother/Yard Sale Woman), Estelle Harris (Mrs. Potato Head), Jodi Benson (Tour Guide Barbie/Barbie on Backpack), Joe Ranft (Wheezy the Penguin/Heimlich the Caterpillar), Andrew Stanton (Evil Emperor Zurg), R. Lee Ermey (Army Sarge), Jonathan Harris (Geri the Toy Cleaner)

Overview

This movie is a sequel to 1995's *Toy Story*. In the first one, the big event was that Buzz discovered he is a mass-produced toy; this time the big event is that Woody discovers he is a collectible and is even famous in some quarters of the world. Though I very much like both movies, I think *Toy Story 2* is more dynamic than the original *Toy Story*, which is why I am including it in this book.

Analysis

Chapter 1: "Opening Titles"

Chapter 2: "Buzz's Mission"

We are watching action-play in the video game "Buzz Lightyear: Attack on Zurg" but do not know it at first. The interesting thing about this sequence in terms of acting is that everything the characters say is sort of fake and melodramatic. In other words, it sounds like bad voice acting. **Stage actors learn early in their careers that one of the most difficult things is to believably portray a bad or stiff actor. Bad actors don't think they are bad actors, which is the challenge.** Even though we do not know we are watching a game, we in the audience get the sense that another shoe is going to drop sometime soon. And it does so when the villainous Zurg blasts Buzz to smithereens.

Chapter 3: "Woody's Lost Hat"

We discover that the "real" Buzz and his buddy Rex the Dinosaur are playing the video game. **Emotion tends to lead to action.** Note how Rex's frustration is expressed physically. When we first see **Woody, he is searching for his hat in the chest of drawers. His behavior is strongly influenced by the pressure of time.** Woody's owner, Andy, is due to leave for cowboy camp momentarily, so there is a lot of urgency. In my acting workshops, I occasionally will demonstrate how the simple act of entering a room can be changed with nothing more than varying the time pressure. A person will move differently if he has a lot of time to complete an action. Also, it is when we get in too big a hurry that we tend to hurt ourselves, which is what happens to Woody when he cascades to the floor. In terms of scene construction, **Woody is playing an action (searching for his hat) in pursuit of an objective (being ready when Andy comes to fetch him for cowboy camp) while overcoming an obstacle (time pressure plus disarray in the room).** Notice that Mrs. Potato Head is reading a book when Mr. Potato Head runs in to tell her he has found her missing ear. The acting note there is that **you should play an action until something happens to make you play a different action.** She is reading the book. He enters and interrupts that, so she shifts to a different action.

Chapter 4: "It's Buster"

The sequence with Buster the dog is delightful. Dogs have their own instinct-based short-term spectrum of thinking and their own brand of emotions. Buster exhausts himself in his search for Woody, and then we have the turnabout in which we in the audience learn it is all a big game. It is wonderful that the dog knows the toys live, but still remains a dog. It would have wrecked everything if the storytellers had opted to let Buster speak words after the toys come to life.

Woody's reaction to being shelved is excellent. I suggest you play it several times slowly and watch the thought process. He first realizes Andy is leaving for camp without him. Then he realizes he has been shelved. Then he checks his arm to see how bad the damage is. Then he realizes all the other toys are watching his misfortune and are feeling sorry for him. He is very sad, and the sadness (emotion) is what leads him to withdraw to the back of the shelf, out of sight. **The more specific the character's thought process, the better the performance.**

Chapter 5: "The Nightmare"

The difference between a dream and a nightmare is that nightmares deal with mortality. In a nightmare, you face your death. That is why you wake up sweating and sometimes even screaming.

Chapter 6: "Wheezy"

This sequence doesn't have a lot of conflict. Mainly, it is an expository way of introducing a new character, Wheezy. For me, the most important part of the scene is the information that Andy's mom lied to him about getting Wheezy's squeaker fixed. Given that Wheezy is probably clinically depressed by the time we meet him, his behavior makes sense. He's looking at his own mortality, which is sort of fitting considering we meet him just after Woody's nightmare.

Chapter 7: "Yard Sale"

Woody rescues Wheezy. Note that his actions change but the objective remains the same. **Play an action until something happens to make you play a different action.** First he calls Buster the dog. Then he tries to climb down from the upper shelf and falls. Once on Buster's back, he has the dog gallop for the yard sale. The objective all along is to rescue Wheezy. The obstacles are several, all with the situation: (1) He's a toy and so has to hide the fact that he lives, (2) his small size makes it difficult to get down off the top shelf in Andy's room, and (3) his arm is ripped, so he has to do everything one-handed. One action is connected to the next up to the point where Woody is accidentally tossed from Buster's back, at which point the objective changes. After he falls and Buster heads inside the front door of the house, Wheezy is officially rescued but Woody is in serious danger. His objective now changes to saving himself. His first new action is to try to run into the house, but he is seen by a human and must instead pretend to be lifeless. The obstacle is that he is a toy and that he is in the open yard instead of the relative safety of Andy's room.

Chapter 8: "Kidnapped!"

This sequence would be **an adrenaline moment for Woody.** He certainly will never forget the day Big Al stole him away from the yard sale.

While Woody is pretending to be a lifeless toy, the action in the scene shifts to negotiations between Al and Andy's mom. Al's objective is to get Woody. His first action is to try to cheat Andy's mom with a low-ball offer. She notices Woody and retrieves him from Al's arms, explaining that he is not for sale. Al's next action is to distract Andy's mom by kicking the skateboard into some toys. While she is distracted, he steals Woody. All of his actions are in pursuit of the same objective. His first conflict/obstacle is with Andy's mom because she doesn't want to sell Woody at any price, not even for $50 and Al's watch. When it is clear that Woody will not be sold, Al's obstacle/conflict changes to conflict with the situation. He changes actions when he steals Woody.

Every character in a scene should be able to answer the question "What am I doing?"—in a theatrical sense. In other words, what action am I playing in pursuit of what objective? And what is the obstacle/conflict? The scenes in this chapter and also in Chapter 7 are brilliantly written. Every character has a life and actions to play. It is worth playing the chapters a couple of times, looking at the action from individual characters' perspectives. Notice how each thought is animated.

Buzz races to Woody's rescue. His objective is to save Woody. His first action is to get from the bedroom down to the front yard. Once there, he has to somehow get in the same vehicle with Woody. His conflict is with his situation. **Remember, a scene is a negotiation and, in every negotiation, there is a way you can win and a way you can lose.** Buzz wins if he successfully gets into the car with Woody and maneuvers further to rescue him. He loses if Al gets away with Woody. As it turns out, Buzz falls off Al's rear bumper into the street. He therefore loses the negotiation.

Chapter 9: "Who Stole Woody?"

Buzz attempts to figure out the code in the license plate. His objective is to crack the code; his action is to try first one set of letters and then another in the decoder; his conflict is with the situation. The conflict resolves itself when Al's Toy Barn comes up on the decoder. After that, all of the characters in the room shift into a new objective and begin more new actions. **Acting should be seamless like this. One action leads to the next and then leads to the next.**

Chapter 10: "The Roundup Gang"

Most of this chapter is exposition. Woody learns of his heritage as the lead character on the TV show *Woody's Roundup Gang*. The most significant note regarding performance in this chapter has to do with Jessie. She is beyond excited that Woody has finally shown up. **Comedy is drama extended, heightened.** She doesn't simply greet Woody enthusiastically, she turns him over and gives him nuggies! She tosses him this way and that. Her emotion is leading her to energetically celebrate. Ask yourself if you, as the animator of this sequence, would have gone quite as far as these animators did with Jessie.

Chapter 11: "Operation Rescue Woody"

The objective is to rescue Woody. The characters, led by Buzz, are all pursuing the same objective. Each of them plays actions according to his or her own character. The conflict is with the situation.

Chapter 12: "Woody's Roundup"

The black-and-white "Woody's Finest Hour" segment of *Woody's Roundup Gang* is awfully clever. Notice that the scene construction within the segment is correct in terms of action, objective, and obstacle, but the degree of seriousness is less because the target audience for the old TV show was little kids. Those old TV shows from the 1950s were corny and full of coincidence and cliffhanger endings.

The scene proceeds with exposition as Woody explores his various trademark toys. The transition comes when the Prospector calls out, "Now, it's on to the museum!" Woody is so jarred by this announcement that he loses his balance on the record player and is tossed on his rear end. Immediately, **he has conflict with the situation, plus the beginnings of conflict with himself.** He will have to decide whether to go to the museum in Japan or return home to Andy. Notice the Prospector's shift in character after Woody explains that his journey began in the yard sale. **The Prospector's objective is to convince Andy to remain with the Roundup Gang. He has both conflict with the situation and conflict with another character (Woody).** His action is to malign the character of Woody's owner, Andy. Jessie also criticizes Andy at this point, but she is not the schemer that the Prospector is. She is more frustrated with the situation than anything else.

Chapter 13: "Woody Loses His Arm"

Woody's traumatic injury sends him into a panic. He is for the moment more vulnerable, both physically and mentally, and so the Prospector attacks. He is trying to wear down Woody's resolve. The pressure increases Woody's conflict with himself and with his situation. Jessie is mad at Woody, and so we have a bit of conflict between those two characters. Remember, a scene is a negotiation. Any of these negotiations I am pointing out have the potential to be resolved. If Andy decides to stay, the Prospector and Jessie win; if he insists on leaving, they lose.

Chapter 14: "Buzz's Speech"

Buzz rallies the troops as they slowly make their way to Al's Toy Barn. I like the way that Slinky is sniffing the ground. All that was minimally necessary was to have him follow Buzz's lead, but the decision was wisely made to keep him in a doglike mode of behavior. Cute. We also learn that the Hamm the Pig has a streak of modesty, which allows us a moment of empathy with him.

Chapter 15: "Getting the Arm"

Woody tries to fetch his lost arm from Al's shirt pocket. He has conflict with the situation—Cheetos on the floor looming like so many orange land mines, Bullseye the horse trying to follow, Al perhaps sleeping lightly, the fact that Woody must do everything with only one arm. If Al wakes up, he will discover Woody a very long way from his glass cage. This all makes for pretty high drama. Action, objective, and obstacle are clear.

The belch gag, in which Woody gets a face full of Al's awful breath, looks to me like it may have been added later in production. There is a slight continuity problem with the way Woody is reaching for his missing arm in Al's pocket. Personally, I don't think the belch was necessary. It reminds me of the Stromboli garlic-breath gag in *Pinocchio*. It actually leads to a bit of weak acting on Woody's part, which is atypical for this movie. His reaction shot to the stench of Al's breath is pushed, and it's a pretty cheap joke. He gasps and gags, takes off his hat, and waves the smell in the other direction. Given the dangerousness of his situation and the possibility that Al might wake up at any moment, I think Woody's larger objective would be to remain undetected. The bad breath would become part of his obstacle. If he were honestly playing a theatrical action instead of clowning for the camera, he would have tried not to move at all. The last thing he wants to do is rouse Al. All that hat flapping is way over the top. Anyway, the reaction to such an odor would be to squint the eyes closed in disgust and to try not to wake Al, not cause the eyes to gape wide in alarm. I think maybe this gag would have been better placed in the outtakes in the closing credits. The bit in which Bullseye is licking Al's fingers, however, is on the money. A horse would do that.

Chapter 16: "Crossing the Road"

The objective is to save Woody. The action is to cross the road. The obstacle is the traffic (conflict with situation). In the negotiation, they win if they get across the road unscathed. They lose if they get squashed.

Chapter 17: "The Cleaner"

Notice how much of the Cleaner's personality is exposed in a thirty-five-second time frame. I will be surprised if the animator for that character did not have an extensive character bible/analysis on him. You really get the impression that the old man has repaired dolls thousands of times and that he is proud of his craft. Notice how his hand searches for the drawer that contains his magnifying glasses. You can feel the man's thinking by the gestures in the hand. Notice the way he casually flips the vise handle to secure Woody in the jaws of the vise. There is a relaxation and assurance in all of his movements. His actions, objectives, and obstacles are clear. Notice the expression on the man's face when Al tries to rush him. You know right away that many people in the past have tried to rush him and he's not having any of it. This is a marvelous sequence from all sorts of perspectives.

Chapter 18: "Al's Toy Barn"

The objective is to save Woody. The action is to get into the store. The obstacle is that the place is overwhelmingly huge. The most significant acting note in this chapter is the way that Rex is distracted by the book on game strategy. **Play an action until something happens to make you play a different action.** In this case, the thing that happened was that Rex noticed the book. It is significant that, as Buzz and the boys fan out into the warehouse, Rex has his head buried in the book. This is probably a necessary bit of business to set up the Zurg sequences later, but Rex's true objective really should still be to rescue Woody. By reading the book while he is walking, it makes his primary objective—at least for the moment—developing tricks to defeat Zurg in the video game. Acting-wise, it is a wee bit inconsistent, but it's not a big deal.

Chapter 19: "Woody's Restoration"

This is more marvelous character work for the Cleaner. I particularly like the moment when he places Woody gently inside the glass case at the end and, almost as an afterthought, adjusts the sheriff's badge on Woody's chest. Everything has to be just so.

Chapter 20: "Buzz Switch"

Buzz wanders into the shelves of new Buzz Lightyear toys. **Play an action until something happens to make you play a different one.** He still has the objective of rescuing Woody but, for a moment, that is upstaged by a shorter-term objective to learn more about the replicas of himself. When New Buzz springs to life, Buzz has conflict with his situation as well as conflict with another character. When he says, "I don't have time for this" and tries to walk away, it is an attempt to resolve the negotiation. It fails.

Chapter 21: "The Barbie Aisle"

The storytellers are having a lot of fun with Barbie dolls in the first half of this chapter. It really doesn't add much to the story, but it's fun to watch. It is also a salute to merchandising.

We get back to the story when New Buzz straps Buzz into the box and takes his place in the car with the other toys. His motivation for getting in the car is to learn the secret of how to defeat Zurg. He of course knows nothing about rescuing Woody. I confess I fretted over this bit of character development. It is a bit of a stretch to think that New Buzz would so readily hop in the car with strangers like that.

Chapter 22: "Jessie's Story" ("When She Loved Me")

The structure of this sequence is interesting because the flashback itself increases the conflict that Woody has with himself. Normally, flashback sequences are a relatively weak storytelling device, but this one works pretty well. Part of the reason is that dolls do not age, and so Jessie is the same age in the flashback that she is in the present moment. The flashback makes more tangible the obvious fact that humans grow up and become adults. It's really a very nice bit of storytelling. After the song is over, we see some excellent acting as Woody struggles with whether or not to return to Andy or remain with the Roundup Gang. It is good storytelling that he opens the heater vent and is literally one step from leaving before the negotiation with himself is resolved.

Chapter 23: "The Toys Find Al"

Rex shares with New Buzz the strategy he has learned for defeating Zurg. Later, New Buzz makes that comment about Al being "an agent of Zurg if I ever saw one." This is intended to be a transitional point for New Buzz because, after this, he joins the other toys in hot pursuit of Al. He is pursuing Al as an agent of Zurg, but the other toys mistakenly believe he is motivated by the objective of rescuing Woody.

Meanwhile, back at the warehouse aisle, Buzz successfully frees himself from the box. Action, objective, and obstacle are clear in that sequence.

Hats off to the storytellers for finding such a clever way to release Zurg into the story. Those electronic doors banging on his box work great.

Chapter 24: "Into the Vents"

Most of this chapter is an extended action sequence. It works because New Buzz does not realize he is a toy and does not in fact possess superpowers. This leads to a lot of funny business and cross-purposes between the characters. New Buzz's bizarre behavior becomes part of the conflict with the situation experienced by the other characters as they pursue their objective of rescuing Woody.

Chapter 25: "Sheriff Woody"

Notice that Woody's power center shifts when he emerges from the box while playing the part of Sheriff Woody. He walks sort of like John Wayne. Power center in the hip. Then, when he gets the idea for the burning-barn scenario, his power center shifts upward, to his chest. As the power center rises higher, his rhythm increases. **A lower power center requires a slower character rhythm. Anxiety is a high and heady power center.** Woody Allen's power center is all above his shoulders.

Chapter 26: "To the Rescue"

This chapter does not have a lot of nuance. It is a big action sequence. The actions are all justified by the objectives, and the conflict in the early part of the scene is with the situation. Once both Buzzes are in the scene at the same time, they have conflict with one another.

Chapter 27: "Woody Stays"

This chapter is chock full of excellent acting. Once it is clear that Woody intends to stay with the Roundup Gang, he has conflict with Buzz. Once Buzz and the other toys depart, the pressure on Woody is intense and the conflict shifts to conflict with self. Woody is struggling with basic values, the things that make life worth living. This is where the shamanistic message of *Toy Story 2* is made evident. What, indeed, is the highest value in life if it is not to be loved? It is worth playing this chapter a couple of times to watch the animation of individual thoughts.

Chapter 28: "Stinky Pete"

The most significant purpose of this chapter is to expose the underlying values of the Prospector. He is a lonely and frustrated old man. In this story, he would be the villain. **A villain is a regular person with a fatal flaw. I would say that the Prospector's fatal flaw is jealousy.** He has been driven near mad during a lifetime of being left on the store shelf. When the Prospector shows his true colors in this scene, Woody is instantly thrown into conflict with another character.

Chapter 29: "Zurg Battle"

There is not a lot of subtle acting in this chapter. Zurg appears and we enter the world of video games again and he and New Buzz stage their climatic battle. The surprising element is that Rex is the one that saves the day, and we learn that Zurg is really New Buzz's father.

Chapter 30: "To the Airport"

Action and more action. Marvelous animation, but the performances are pretty straightforward. Actions, objectives, and obstacles are clear. The toys are still saving Woody.

Chapter 31: "Woody vs. Prospector"

Woody and the Prospector fight to the finish on the conveyor belt. With the help of his friends, Woody prevails. **Acting is**

reacting. Note the Prospector's reaction when he is sentenced to "the true meaning of playtime."

Chapter 32: "Saving Jessie"

This is an homage to a hundred westerns, and I love it. Woody is a true hero, risking life and limb to save the damsel in distress. **Note that when Woody opens the trunk to save Jessie, we discover her in the fetal position.** That is a nicely observed bit of performance. The animator could have just tossed her in there like a rag doll. **The fetal position carries a lot of visual and empathetic energy to the viewer.**

Chapter 33: "Take Off!"

The movie crescendos here as Woody, with the help of the other hero in this movie, Buzz Lightyear, saves Jessie at the very last moment.

Chapter 34: "Welcome Home"

My favorite moment in this chapter is Buzz's reaction when Jessie flies across the room to open the door so the dog can go out. Romance is in the air.

Chapter 35: End Credits

8. Spirited Away

Walt Disney (2002)

Chief Executive Producer: Yasuyoshi Tokuma

Executive Producers: Toshio Suzuki, Takeyoshi Matsushita, Seiichiro Ujiie, Yutaka Narita, Koji Hoshino, Banjiro Uemura, Hironori Aihara

Original Story and Screenplay: Hayao Miyazaki

Director: Hayao Miyazaki

Art Director: Yoji Takeshige

Editor: Takeshi Seyama

Director of Digital Animation: Mitsunori Kataama

Digital Animators: Yoichi Senzui, Masaru Karube, Miki Sato, Hiroki Yamada, Yuji Tone

Animators: Masashi Ando (supervising animator), Kitaro Kosaka (supervising animator), Megumi Kagawa (supervising animator), Takeshi Inamura, Kenichi Yamada, Masaru Matsuse, Hideaki Yoshio, Eiji Yamamori, Katsutoshi Nakamura, Kazuyoshi Onoda, Makiko Suzuki, Mariko Matsuo, Atsushi Tamura, Hiromasa Yonebayashi, Kaori Fujii, Tamami Yamada, Makiko Futaki, Yoshiyuki Momose, Akihiko Yamashita, Nobuyuki Takeuchi, Shogo Furuya, Misuzu Kurata, Atsushi Yamagata, Shigeru Kimishima, Kiroomi Yamakawa, Nobuhiro Osugi, Yuichi Tanaka, Shizue Kaneko, Hideki Hamasu, Hisaki Furukawa, Kenichi Konishi, Masaru

Oshiro, Shinya Ohira, Shinji Hashimoto, Hisashi Nakayama, Noboru Takano, Masako Shinohara, Kuniyuki Ishii, Shojuro Yamauchi

Voice Cast (English Language): Daveigh Chase (Chihiro), Suzanne Pleshette (Yubaba/Zeniba), Jason Marsden (Haku), Susan Egan (Lin), David Ogden Stiers (Kamaji), Lauren Holly (Chihiro's Mother), Michael Chiklis (Chihiro's Father), John Ratzenberger (Assistant Manager), Tara Strong (Baby Boh)

Overview

Hayao Miyazaki, cofounder of Studio Ghibli in Japan, is considered by many people to be the Shakespeare of animation. He is a grand master storyteller, an animator's animator. Among his legions of fans is John Lasseter, head of Pixar Animation Studios. Every new animator should study Miyazaki's work very closely. His animation is not the kind of simple manga-turned-anime that might turn up on Saturday morning television. Japanese animation has a different look and feel than Western animation, it is true, but the acting principles are exactly the same.

Even better for the purposes of this book, Miyazaki is famously hands-on with his movies. He designs all of the characters, makes up his stories, writes the scripts, and polishes the animation. Therefore, we can more easily credit him specifically with the performance we see on-screen. I have watched *Spirited Away* at least fifteen times, and every time I see it again, I see things I didn't see the time before. Every time I think I understand its depth, I discover that it gets deeper—and simpler. We are very fortunate to have Hayao Miyazaki and his talented team of artists at Studio Ghibli among us.

I usually do not much care for English dubbing on foreign films. I prefer to hear the original language and read subtitles. In the case of *Spirited Away*, however, the English dubbing, which was personally directed by John Lasseter of Pixar, is excellent.

Analysis

Chapter 1: Opening Credits/ "The Middle of Nowhere"

The first time we meet ten-year old Chihiro, she is pouting. Her family is moving to a new city and she doesn't like it at all. She is missing her friends and her old school. **Immediately, she has conflict with her situation. Now, since a scene is a negotiation, it is worth also mentioning that her pouting is in itself a strategy. In a negotiation, there must be a way you can win and a way you can lose.** In a child's mind, if she can act up enough, then maybe she will get her own way. In reality, there is not a chance that the family will turn around and go back to their old home. Chihiro realizes this on some level, but she will continue to pout anyway as a negotiating ploy.

Chihiro is terrified when her father, uncharacteristically, begins to speed on the dirt road. **We empathize with her fear.** She feels out of control and she clings to the back seat for stability, crying out that her dad should slow down. The act of clinging is spurred by the emotion of fear. **Emotion tends to lead to action.**

They can drive no further. Father, mother, and Chihiro get out of the car and we have another negotiation at the entrance to the strange building. Notice how Chihiro clings to her father's arm as she tries to persuade him not to go any further? But even with his strength to support her, she wants no part of this odd place. It gives her the creeps. When Dad insists on exploring, Chihiro is in direct conflict with him and tries to win by yelling "Forget it! I'm not going!" and returning to the car. She loses the negotiation, however, and must chase after her parents to catch up. It is better to be with them in a spooky place than it is to be alone in the car. **Note that when Chihiro catches up to her parents she grabs her mother's arm with both hands. That is a gesture motivated by fear.** As I watched this sequence, I marveled at Miyazaki's firm understanding of child psychology. Significantly, Dad did not physically force Chihiro to accompany him into the building. He seemed content to go without her if that is what it took. It seemed that his higher value was to explore. It upstaged his own parental feelings. This would of course scare the daylights out of a ten-year-old girl. The very idea that a parent does not care if you come or go is existentially frightening.

When Chihiro's father follows the aroma of the food (**play an action until something happens to make you play a different action**), he actually begins to run. This is also odd behavior and helps increase the feeling of fear in Chihiro and, by way of empathy, us in the audience. Think about it: if you smell even the most aromatic food, do you run toward it? Maybe a child would, but Chihiro's father is in his mid-thirties. Since emotion tends to lead to action, we can presume that his emotion—whatever it is—is extremely powerful.

Later, after her brief encounter on the bridge with Haku, Chihiro finds the overstuffed pigs sitting where her parents were. This is a nightmarish sequence. Miyazaki has a firm understanding of the fears of children. Parental abandonment and the possible loss of personal identity loom large in *Spirited Away.*

Regarding Haku, we do not initially empathize with him because he is a spirit. He does not appear to have normal human emotions, and his eyes have been purposely made to appear "strange." (See *The Art of Spirited Away* by Mayou Mizaki, Viz Communications, 2002.) Remember, we humans empathize only with emotion. To the degree that a character does not appear to have emotion, we will view him in a more cerebral way.

Chapter 2: "It's Just a Dream"

At the water's edge, Chihiro struggles to "wake up" from a bad dream. She is starting to become invisible and can see through her own hands. This is brilliant storytelling. To disappear is to die. Notice that Chihiro crouches into a kind of fetal position and tries to comfort herself. The single close-up shot of her feet in tennis shoes rocking back and forth is powerful emotionally. She is terrified. Emotion leads to action. The action is to comfort herself.

When she runs up the hill, note that she slips and regains her balance. It happens quickly but helps underline that she is on slippery reality. All the animators really had to do was to get her up the hill, right? But they added that slip and recovery. That is good animation.

Haku rescues Chihiro by giving her food from the spirit world. This will stop her from disappearing. Chihiro has a terrible negotiation at that moment. She does not know what the substance is that Haku is trying to feed her and she has every reason to be suspicious at this moment. On the other hand, she is disappearing (dying) fast. She is stuck between a rock and a hard place. This is conflict with the situation. She eats the food, thereby resolving the negotiation. As it turns out, she wins that negotiation because she again becomes whole.

The next major negotiation in this chapter occurs when Haku tells Chihiro that she must adventure into the bathhouse alone. She cries out, "I don't want to be alone!" He presents the case to her: If you want to rescue your parents, you will have to be alone. Again, she is between a rock and a hard place. Conflict with the situation. She resolves it by deciding to be courageous. She will go into the bathhouse alone.

Chapter 3: "Finding Work at the Bathhouse"

What child has not fallen down stairs at one time or another? The stairs at the bathhouse are several stories high, are very steep, and have no handrails. Again, Miyazaki taps into a child's deepest fears. It is easy for us to empathize with Chihiro. When the step broke, sending her careening downward, my heart skipped a beat.

Once she is inside the bathhouse, Chihiro meets Kamaji, the six-armed old man that runs the boiler room. The sight of a six-armed man further frightens Chihiro, and we empathize with her fear. She flattens herself against the boiler room wall, trying to hide while figuring out what to do. Note the degree of tension in her body as she pushes against the wall. Then she screws up her courage and pushes forward like the heroine she is.

Her dialogue with Kamaji emphasizes the conflict she has with her situation. As gruff as the old man appears, he immediately displays a soft underbelly. Chihiro is not really threatened by him once she gets used to the six arms.

Chapter 4: "Meeting Yubaba"

When Chihiro is taken to meet Yubaba, she turns to thank Kamaji for his help and bangs her head on the top of the passageway doorframe. She is in continual danger of hurting herself, it seems. This little bump on the head would be easy to overlook, but I am encouraging you to think about it a moment. The animators did not have to include that. It was only necessary to get Chihiro out of the boiler room. **The emotional impact of her banging her head was startling. The moment passes quickly, but it is effective. Miyazaki's filmmaking is chock full of this type of minor moment if you look. This really helps define character and establish atmosphere and mood.**

The first couple of elevators to the top floor are almost as dangerous as the steep outside steps Chihiro had to navigate earlier. There is no protective cage on them. Again, the little girl flattens herself against a wall in a gesture of fear and self-protection.

Note the diversionary sequence between Lin and Frog. The scene construction is conflict between characters. The negotiation is over who gets to eat the roasted newt. Lin wins.

Once Chihiro arrives at Yubaba's quarters, the atmosphere changes. Now we have elegant carpets and a warm fireplace. It is almost comforting until those bodiless heads start bouncing around the room. I personally thought those heads were just about the most disturbing characters in the movie. Real nightmare fodder.

Yubaba takes possession of Chihiro's name, calling her Sen instead. This plays into a child's fear of disappearing. You lose your name and you lose your identity. (Personal aside: When I was a young boy, my mother remarried and my stepfather adopted me, changing my last name to Hooks. I was given the option of also changing my first name as long as we were going through the legal process of name changing anyway. The idea of changing my first name was traumatic to me. I was Ed, after all. I was not a Nick or Dave. My very identity was at stake. This is the psychology that is in play with this sequence between Chihiro and Yubaba.)

Chapter 5: "Sen's New Life"

The sequence between Sen (Chihiro) and Haku outside the pig barn is fascinating. He gives her food on which he has cast a spell, explaining that it will restore her strength. After she takes two or three bites, she begins to weep. I spent some time trying to figure out how the acting is working. What is she crying about specifically? An emotion can be defined as an automatic value response. Her tears are being driven by an emotion of some kind, but I'm not sure what it is. She might be in a kind of shock. It could not possibly be that her energy had fallen to a level where she was incapable of tears because she was crying in her bed only a short while earlier. It seems to me these are tears of relief rather than pain, perhaps similar to the kinds of tears one sheds at a wedding. A psychiatrist explained to me once that people cry at weddings because the events involve both hope (a new life together) and loss (childhood is over). He said the contrast between the two can evoke tears because the emotions are so strong. Ask yourself when was the last time you saw tears of this sort in an animated film. It is most unusual and is very arresting. It makes sense that Miyazaki would be the one to do it first. I really do think that if this man ever decides to give up animation, he would make a marvelous psychologist.

Chapter 6: "We Have an Intruder"

Note how Chihiro repeatedly slips and falls from the bathtub. Each time the falls are pretty tough. Ask yourself why the animators had her fall so many times. A single fall might have sufficed to establish that the surface of the tub was slimy and slippery, yes? I think the repeated falls keep Chihiro in constant conflict with her situation. It helps keeps the tension high.

The negotiation between No Face and Chihiro over the bath tokens is interesting. If she accepts the offer, No Face wins the negotiation and will eat her. But she is not greedy. She only takes what she needs. That is why No Face disappears and drops the tiles to the floor. He lost.

The Stink Spirit sequence is wonderful for the way it capitalizes on the sense of smell. Miyazaki has not simply made the Stink Spirit smell bad; he has made him smell sickening—and he has even worked in an environmental warning because the source of the odor is the tossed-off debris of civilization. Chihiro has to overcome her revulsion in order to serve the Spirit and to further her quest toward saving her parents. She is in conflict with her situation. The obstacle is the stench. She loses if she runs away, and she wins if she can successfully give the Stink Spirit his bath.

Chapter 7: "Working for Tips"

The primary purpose of this chapter is to define the penalties of greed. No Face has the power to create whatever someone wants the most. In the case of the bathhouse workers, it is gold. As soon as they realize he has the capacity to create gold out of thin air, they begin treating him with extreme deference. From their perspective, the negotiation is with the situation. They think that the more they cater to the spirit, the more gold they get. From No Face's perspective, it is a matter of establishing the degree of greed. He wins if his victims cave into greed and take the gold. Significantly, Chihiro does not accept the gold when it is offered to her.

Chapter 8: "A Strange Visit to the Nursery"

Chihiro's objective is to save Haku, who has flown into the top-most window of the bathhouse. Her obstacle is that there is no easy way up. She has to climb the outside of the building, walking along rusted pipes, risking her life. The negotiation is that if she falls, she loses; if she successfully gets to Haku, she wins.

Chihiro's scenes with Baby are just about the strangest in the movie in my opinion. A baby that huge is almost a living oxymoron in the first place. Baby talks like an adult but has the maturity of a child. We feel zero empathy for Baby, despite his (her?) cries. Baby's emotions seem calculated rather than heartfelt. The most significant aspect of Chihiro's encounters with Baby is the way she stands up to the large child. Notice the moment when she holds her bloody palm up for Baby to see. ("Germs! I got germs, see?") That is smart thinking on Chihiro's part, and it doesn't come from fear. She is using her head. I perceive growth in her character in this chapter.

We are also learning some new story points, having to do with how Haku got the Golden Seal from Yubaba's sister, Zeniba.

Chapter 9: "The Golden Seal"

The action sequences in which Chihiro rides on Haku's back as he writhes through space and crashes into Kamaji's boiler room are nothing short of majestic animation. All of the action is emotion driven.

After Haku returns to his human form and is near death, Chihiro makes the decision to return the golden seal to Zeniba. This is a pure act of courage and love. Haku helped her at one time, and she wants now to help him. This is not the thinking of a young ten-year-old girl. She is showing signs of real maturity. She is no longer trembling with fear when she confronts an obstacle, but is acting from strength.

Chapter 10: "A Monster Called No Face"

Chihiro bravely faces the monster No Face. Note that she peacefully sits in his roaring presence and speaks to him calmly. Compare this kind of behavior with the way she behaved back in Chapters 1, 2, and 3.

After she feeds No Face the food from the River Spirit, causing him to purge and rage into a fury, Chihiro flees. No Face is in hot pursuit. I do not interpret her running away to be a sign of cowardice, however. Fear is a normal and healthy emotion even in mature people. Her flight is motivated by emotion and, acting-wise, it is correct. The flight through the bathhouse is another example of marvelously detailed animation. There are many characters being knocked out of the way. Play the sequence a couple of times and you will see personality and solid acting in each of them.

One note about the way No Face purges. Most of us would call it vomiting and, if you stop to think about it, that is a perfect way of expressing the expulsion of evil. As vile as vomiting may be, there is still something satisfying and cleansing about it once it is done. Even children—the target audience for this movie—will understand that on a primal level.

Chapter 11: "The Train to Swamp Bottom"

There is a shot of Chihiro on the train, after all of the other passengers have gotten off, and her little spirit friends are asleep in her lap. She looks out the window and is deep in thought. The moment is very still and very full, and it lasts a couple of seconds. Freeze frame on that shot and study her face. Note that it is actually longer, a different shape than it had at the beginning of the movie. It has more definition. Compare this shot to the shot of her face in Chapter 2 when she sees the spirit ship approaching and cries out, "I'm dreaming! I'm dreaming!" Freeze on that close-up. Then go back to Chapter 11. This is very subtle and effective character development. Most people would not notice the evolution of her facial shape.

Chapter 12: "What Did You Do with My Baby?"

Haku negotiates with Yubaba for the return of Baby. Conflict between characters. Haku wins, but Yubaba drives a hard bargain.

Chapter 13: "A Visit with Zeniba"

Zeniba turns out to be the granny we all wish we had. She's a fool for love and has a weakness for brave little girls. Most of this chapter is resolution. There is some low-grade negotiation between Chihiro and Zeniba, but it is one-sided. Chihiro has nothing more to give on her side of the negotiation. She doesn't know it yet, but she has already won.

Isn't Haku majestic in his dragon form? When Chihiro rushed to embrace him, I could swear I saw him smile. I felt a rush of empathy for him.

Chapter 14: "Finding the Way Home"

Haku learns his true identity and the beginnings of his relationship with Chihiro. Notice the difference in his eyes once he remembers. There are no negotiations in this brief chapter. It is all resolution.

Chapter 15: "One Final Test"

I like the pacing when Chihiro walks alone toward Yubaba. She is going to take the final test. Notice how erect her back is, how firm her step is. Even from an aerial shot you can see the strength. The fearful and sulky child at the beginning of the movie is going to be a fine adult one day. The final line of the movie tells it all. "I think," says Chihiro, "I can handle it."

9. The Emperor's New Groove

Walt Disney Pictures (2000)

Producers: Randy Fullmer (producer), Don Hahn (executive producer), Patricia Hicks (associate producer)

Director: Mark Dindal

Writers: Roger Allers (story), Mark Dindal (story), Matthew Jacobs (story), David Reynolds (screenplay), Chris Williams (story)

Editors: Tom Finan, Pam Ziegenhagen

Art Directors: Colin Stimpson, Thomas Cardone

Animators: Pierre Alary, Tim Allen (Kuzco/Kuzco Llama), Dale Baer (supervising animator Yzma), James Baker (animator Kuzco/Kuzco Llama), Tony Bancroft (supervising animator Kronk), Jared Beckstrand (animator Pacha), David Block (animator Kronk), Borja Montoro Cavero (animator), Jerry Yu Ching (animator Kuzco/Kuzco Llama), Sandro Cleuzo (lead animator The Song Guy/Waitress/Old Man/Officials/Maidens), Bob Davies (animator Kronk), Patrick Delage (animator), Eric Delbecq (animator), Roberto Espanto Domingo (animator Yzma), Marc Eoche-Duval (animator), Brian Ferguson (animator), Douig Frankel (lead animator Chicha),

Tom Gately (animator Pacha), Eric Gervais-Despres (scene planner), Thierry Goulard (animator), David Hancock (animator Pacha), Clay Kaytis (animator Pacha), Sang-Jin Kim (animator Kuzco/Kuzco Llama), Bert Klein (animator Pacha), Jennifer Cardon Klein (animator Kuzco/Kuzco Llama), James Lopez (animator), Mark Mitchell (animator Kuzco/Kuzco Llama), Joe Oh (animator Kuzco/Kuzco Llama), Jamie Oliff (animator Kuzco/Kuzco Llama), Catherine Poulain (animator), Mark Pudleiner (animator Kuzco/Kuzco Llama), Nik Ramieri (supervising animator Kuzco/Kuzco Llama), Mike Show (animator Nina), Bruce W. Smith (supervising animator Pacha), Marc Smith (animator Kuzco/Kuzco Llama), Chad Stewart (animator Yzma), Michael Stocker (animator Kronk), JC Tran-Quang-Thieu (animator), Steven Wahl (animator Yzma), Andreas Wessel-Therhorn (animator Kuzco/ Kuzco Llama), Theresa Wiseman (animator Pacha), Anthony Ho Wong (animator Pacha), Phil Young (animator Kuzco/ Kuzco Llama)

Voice Cast: David Spade (Kuzco), John Goodman (Pacha), Eartha Kitt (Yzma), Patrick Warburton (Kronk), Wendie Malick (ChiCha), Kellyann Kelso (Chaca)

Overview

The Emperor's New Groove was in development at Disney for a very long time, being known for a while by the title *Kingdom of the Sun*. The original story was about a prince who changes places with someone in his kingdom who looks almost identical to him except for this single mark from the sun. During the developmental process, plot lines were reportedly added and dropped and the idea behind the movie evolved into what we now have before us. *The Emperor's New Groove* was one of several high-budget box-office disappointments that ultimately influenced Disney Animation to abandon 2-D in favor of mainly 3-D production in its feature films.

Analysis

Chapter 1: "The Name Is Kuzco"

We have a very excellent acting lesson in the very beginning, concerning the way Kuzco searches for cover in a rainstorm.

The Llama is miserable and alone in the midst of a gloomy and oppressive tropical jungle. A couple of seconds after he appears on screen, a flash of lightning frightens him and he reacts with a big startled jump. His eyes pop open wide with fear. That is excellent acting. Then the rain starts falling heavily and he moves to a nearby dry space under a large tree frond. That works well too because **a scene is a negotiation and his objective is to protect himself from the rain. He wins if he finds a dry place, and he loses if he gets wet. He has conflict with his situation.** Once Kuzco is in the dry spot, however, water overflows the frond and douses him. Now, pay close attention to what happens next:

Logically, his objective would still be to find a dry space, yes? His action should arguably be to look for yet another possible spot of refuge in case things get even worse. But Kuzco gives up the quest because he is already wet from the frond-douse. He crawls directly back out into the rain, lies down in the most unprotected spot, where he knows for certain he will get even more soaked—and assumes the fetal position.

It appears to me that the action in this sequence was designed to elicit sympathy for the Llama at the very top of the movie, and that is what we have accomplished. We have learned that the Llama's spirit is low, that he appears depressed, and that he has evidently given up fighting the good fight. We feel sorry for him.

In this book, I have spoken several times about the differences between sympathy (feeling for) and empathy (feeling into) and the trouble storytellers can encounter when they get the concepts mixed up. It is okay to elicit sympathy for a character at times, but you had better be very careful about how you do it. We humans act to survive and we respond favorably when we see other humans trying to survive. When we see a character who has evidently *stopped* acting to survive, which is the case in this opening sequence, the behavior distances us from him rather than drawing us to him.

By the way, the setup for this scene is similar to one in Shakespeare's *The Tempest*. In act 2, scene 2 the jester Trinculo is looking for a place to hide from a tropical storm. Like Kuzco, Trinculo is a pampered person who is not accustomed to being in the elements.

Chapter 2: "Main Title—'Perfect World'"

Expository/connective sequence during which we meet the human Kuzco and learn that he is spoiled rotten and can have whatever he wants. He has no regard or respect for those who serve him. In the bonus extras (character voices), producer Randy Fullmer describes Kuzco as having "no patience, arrogant, all-about-me, snide—but there is a little bit of a charm there, too." Given that we are being asked to spend an hour and a half with this character, I think this is a troublesome setup. Personally, if I run into someone who has no patience and is arrogant, all-about-me, and snide, I'm not going to stick around long enough to find out if he also happens to be charming.

Chapter 3: "Choosing a Bride"

Kuzco insults all of the potential brides.

Note the reaction of the brides after he insults them. The reactions happen pretty much in the background so you'll have to specifically focus on them. If Kuzco is life-or-death powerful, I doubt seriously the rejected brides would be so over the top with their anger. The third one from the left actually looks like she's going to slug him.

Chapter 4: "Pacha Arrives at the Palace"

Expository sequence in which we meet Pacha. We learn something else awful about Kuzco's values. The old man who threw off the emperor's groove (". . . the rhythm in which he lives his life. His pattern of behavior, I threw it off . . .") was physically tossed out a window at Kuzco's instruction. What kind of guy do you have to be to order old men tossed out windows? Here we are on our way into Chapter 5, and I find myself not liking the lead character at all.

Chapter 5: "The Emperor's Adviser"

Yzma (voiced by Eartha Kitt) is, in my view, the most successful characterization in *The Emperor's New Groove*. She reminds me a lot of Cruella de Vil, the classic villain from *101 Dalmatians*. Yzma is hungry for power and afflicted by the fatal flaw of vanity. In this chapter, we see her bully a peasant and then kiss up to the emperor. She has conflict with her situation (not powerful enough) and with other characters—first the peasant and then the emperor. After Kuzco fires her, she is inflamed and infuriated. We know right away that she will fight back—i.e., she will act to survive.

Kronk is a big dumb guy. He is so dumb that he is funny. I like Kronk a lot of the time, but it is worth mentioning that, in life, **stupid people do not think they are stupid.** The first time we see Kronk, he swats a fly on his own head, knocking himself on the floor. I understand this is animation, but even in animation character behavior should be rooted in truth. I probably would have been more amused by the scene if Kronk had swatted the fly, making a squashy mess all over his forehead. That would have been more of a Charlie Chaplin moment.

Chapter 6: "Kuzcotopia"

The emperor intends to demolish Pacha's mountain-top village and replace it with a royal summer retreat. There is some conflict in his encounter with Pacha, but there is not a negotiation. Therefore, the scene structure is weak. **In any negotiation, there must be a way you can win and a way you can lose.** Kuzco has nothing at stake. He holds all the cards and cannot possibly lose the hand.

Chapter 7: "Yzma's Revenge"

Yzma is in conflict with her situation. Her objective is power. The obstacle is Kuzco. She therefore decides to kill Kuzco. Wonderful stuff.

Chapter 8: "To the Secret Lab"

This is mostly a fantasy sequence, but it's fun because Yzma is such an extreme character and because she takes unfettered joy in executing her diabolical plans. There is no particular negotiation to speak of, however. The thrill ride she and Kronk take down the long slide has nothing to do with anything, and I don't know why it is in the movie.

Chapter 9: "A Diabolical Dinner"

Yzma's attempt to poison Kuzco goes awry. Instead of killing the emperor, Kronk manages to turn him into a llama. From a performance perspective, Yzma's objective is to kill Kuzco. Her obstacle is Kronk's ineptitude. Kronk gets the poisons mixed up and so Yzma loses this particular negotiation.

There is an acting lesson in a small moment with Kronk. It only lasts one second, so you'll have to focus in on it: Yzma instructs Kronk to take Kuzco "out of town and finish the job . . . now!" There is a brief beat and then Kronk's eyes go up and to the left, like he just thought of something. "What about dinner?" he asks. In terms of performance, it was not necessary to have his eyes go up that way. I'm sure the intent was to show how dumb Kronk is, but he would actually have appeared dumber if he had taken the brief thinking-beat and then simply asked the question, maybe so as not to offend Yzma. It is not necessary to continually show how dumb Kronk is. It has been established that he is not the brightest bulb on the tree. The key from here on out is to have him do dumb things that he thinks are smart.

Chapter 10: "Finishing the Job"

In order to make this sequence work, Kuzco should arguably have been awake in the bag, not unconscious. Kronk tosses the bag into the water and walks away. Then it occurs to him that the bag is going to plunge over the waterfall, killing Kuzco in a big splash. What is it that causes him to stop and think about the big plunge? There is no noise coming from the bag and Kuzco is now focused on his next action, which is probably to return to Yzma. **The acting principle is that a character should play an action until something happens to make him play a different action.** What is it that motivates him to stop and reconsider the murder? His conscience? I contend it would have been a stronger acting moment if Kuzco had been revived by the plunge into the cold water and began thrashing in the bag, maybe even coughing from the water he is swallowing. Kronk would have heard that commotion and felt pity. The pity would lead to the indecision, reconsideration, and debate between his good and bad angels.

An effective acting moment should appear to the audience to be totally unexpected and simultaneously inevitable. When the audience sees Kronk's attack of conscience, they will mentally replay everything they know about the character, looking for hints that he is the type that might have such attacks of conscience. So far, all we know about Kronk is that he is a taco short of a combo plate. I do not think it is enough to suggest that a person has attacks of conscience simply because he is stupid.

Chapter 11: "Pacha Returns Home"

The sequence between Pacha and his wife, Chicha, and their children is connective and does not have much conflict. There is a slight negotiation with the kids over the terms of going to bed. Later, as Chicha washes dishes, we can see that Pacha is in conflict with himself and with his situation.

The effect of atmosphere on performance is quite nice in this sequence. Michael Chekov talks a lot about the uses of atmosphere in his book *On the Technique of Acting* (Harper Resource, 1991). A warm and cozy and loving home is truly something to fight for. The atmosphere in the home is affecting the behavior of the characters.

Chapter 12: "Demon Llama"

Pacha tells Kuzco he will help him find the way home if Kuzco will agree not to build Kuzcotopia on this particular mountaintop. This is a strong negotiation, and it tells a lot about Pacha's underlying strength and devotion to his family. He knows full well that Kuzco is a dangerous man if crossed and yet he still tries to strike a bargain with him.

As Kuzco disappears down the path, we see Pacha waver. Maybe he should accompany Kuzco to safety after all? It is a moment of foreshadowing, setting up the rescue of Kuzco two chapters from now.

Chapter 13: "Into the Jungle"

We can empathize with Kuzco's fear of the jungle. Performance-wise, this chapter works quite well. **Emotion tends to lead to action. He is afraid and so he careens this way and that, trying to find safety.** Contrast this to the behavior of the llama in that opening sequence.

Chapter 14: "Pacha to the Rescue"

The action sequence in which Pacha swings in à la Tarzan and rescues Kuzco from the jaws of death is very nice. I like the way he missed Kuzco on the first swing and picked him up on the return. Reminded me a bit of Road Runner cartoons.

Kuzco is touched when Pacha gently places his poncho over him to protect him from the cold night. Good acting.

Chapter 15: "The Transition to Power"

Yzma takes over the throne. This is an expository sequence with no real conflict or negotiation until she learns that Kuzco is still alive. At that point, Yzma has conflict with her situation.

Chapter 16: "Bad Dreams"

I suppose the reason for this sequence is to establish that Pacha's wife was the one who told him to go find the emperor. We can presume that Pacha did not tell her that the emperor is currently a llama, but he must have told her about the emperor's plan to build Kuzcotopia on the mountaintop. It is hard to be certain. The kids are cute and mama is maternal and comforting, but there isn't any real negotiation taking place in the sequence.

Chapter 17: "An Apparent Change of Heart"

Kuzco is evidently so touched by Pacha's good nature and generosity that he agrees not to build Kuzcotopia on Pacha's home mountain. The sequence between the two of them at the water's edge is excellent in terms of negotiation and subtext. Given what a jerk Kuzco has been up to this point in the movie, however, it is hard to believe he would experience a 180-degree change of heart based on the fact that Pacha gave him a blanket in the cold night.

Chapter 18: "Battle at the Bridge"

Kuzco is still a jerk, and it turns out he was lying about his promise not to build Kuzcotopia. In terms of performance, everything works well in this chapter. Both characters play actions until something happens to make them play different actions. The negotiations are clear. The weakness is in the script. Even for such a self-involved character as Kuzco, it is hard to buy that he values the construction of Kuzcotopia over the life of a man who has just saved his life.

Chapter 19: "In Hot Pursuit"

There is a nice lesson in comedy here when Yzma emerges from the carriage and gets her shoes stuck in the mud. **Drama has to do with man's potential; comedy has to do with his limitations.** Yzma may be the most powerful person in the kingdom right now, but her shoes will still get stuck in the mud, and the swarm of bees will still chase her. At the end of the day, she is still human, and that is the source of the gags in this sequence.

After the Yzma mud sequence, we discover that Kronk evidently can talk to squirrels. It's not particularly funny and contains zero negotiation, but the storytellers were looking for some device that would put Yzma and Kronk on the trail of Kuzco. It was convenient to have the squirrel point the way, and you couldn't do that unless you could talk to squirrels. It is not credible, which is the problem. If Kronk was going to talk to squirrels, it would have been stronger to establish that skill in an earlier scene so it would not be so jarring now.

Chapter 20: "Mudka's Meat Hut"

This chapter has a lot of the elements of a French farce with characters running in and out of revolving doors. Pacha has conflict with his situation once he learns that Yzma and Kronk are hunting for Kuzco. His behavior during most of this chapter makes good sense acting-wise. His objective is to save Kuzco, and the obstacle is that Kuzco will not listen to him. Yzma does not have any direct conflict for the entire chapter. In general, she is still in conflict with her situation and is searching for Kuzco so she can kill him. But within the chapter's sequences, it is revolving doors and sight gags.

The primary story development information that is exposed in this chapter is the fresh estrangement between Pacha and Kuzco. At the very end of the chapter, Kuzco overhears Yzma scheming to kill him and seems disillusioned for some reason. That doesn't make a lot of sense given that he fired Yzma in Chapter 5. He already knew she was a problem. Anyway, his being in a physical location so that he can overhear her depends upon coincidence. You need to be very careful about how you use coincidence as a storytelling device. See *Story: Substance,*

Structure, Style, and the Principles of Screenwriting by Robert McKee, HarperCollins, 1997, pp. 356–59.

Chapter 21: "A Llama Alone"

Kuzco is sad because Pacha is no longer at his side and because he has no friends back at the palace. He is feeling sorry for himself. The location turns back into the same swamp in which we found Kuzco in Chapter 1.

Kuzco has conflict with his situation, but the problem is that he is not doing anything to solve it. He is playing the part of a victim. **There is a big difference between being a victim and being victimized. If you portray your character as a victim, you run the strong risk that you will lose the empathetic response of your audience. Humans act to survive. We want to see characters do something to survive, even if the choice is wrong.** When Kuzco lies down in the pouring rain and says, "Leave me alone," he is giving up. He is not acting to survive, and so we in the audience emotionally distance ourselves from him.

Chapter 22: "Good News"

When Yzma sits up in bed, she has cucumber slices on her eyes. That is a wonderful character element! Her fatal flaw is vanity. The fact that she would sleep on her back with cucumber slices balanced on her eyes tells us volumes about the degree of her vanity. Very nice!

Chapter 23: "Friends, Finally"

Kuzco learns, hopefully once and for all, that love is the highest value. It is worth even more than power and Kuzcotopia with a waterslide. Pacha is sticking with him through thick and thin, regardless of how much or how often Kuzco insults and threatens him.

A good acting lesson to focus on in this chapter is that **a character needs a reason for entering a scene.** At the top of the sequence, Kuzco enters dejectedly. What is his objective, do you think? To make friends with the herd of llamas? It's hard to say. Mainly, he just looks depressed. He appears to be aimlessly wandering. **A character should be able to answer the question "What am I doing?" 100 percent of the time. It is not enough to say "I am wandering around." "Wandering around" is not a theatrical action. Theatrical action is not the same thing as simple behavior. It must have purpose. Acting is playing an action in pursuit of objective while overcoming an obstacle.**

When Kuzco sees Pacha sitting amidst the herd of llamas, there is a nice transition. **You play an action until something happens to make you play a different action.** Seeing Pacha is the thing that causes Kuzco to play a different action.

Chapter 24: "Playtime at Pacha's"

This chapter is full of silly stuff that is fun to watch. Kronk's jump rope sequence is funny if dumb. The negotiations in the scene are (1) between Yzma and Chicha, who intuitively is suspicious of Yzma's true identity and motives, and (2) between Yzma and Chicha when it becomes clear that Chicha does in fact know where Pacha is.

I love the zany Warner Brothers cartoon feel to Yzma's careening trip down the mountain side, terminating when she becomes a human piñata. Very nice animation. It also reminds me once again of Cruella de Vil in *101 Dalmatians.*

Chapter 25: "The Chase"

The moment when the airborne Kronk and Yzma get struck by lightning and tumble from the sky looks like a tribute to Wile E. Coyote in Road Runner cartoons. The timing on that sequence is sharp. **To reiterate the lesson about comedy, it may be true that Yzma can fly in her Kronk-mobile, but she can still get struck by lightning and fall from the sky. Comedy deals with our human limitations.**

Chapter 26: "The Final Showdown"

The extended action sequences in which Yzma, Pacha, and Kuzco compete for possession of the magic vial are based on conflict with situation and conflict between characters. It is a madcap series of sequences that works well from a performance point of view. It seems to me that this is a weak way to resolve the story, though. At the end of the day, it would have been stronger if Kuzco had outwitted Yzma. The way it is constructed, the resolution depends largely on coincidence.

Chapter 27: "A Whole New Groove"

Kuzco is a changed man. Kronk becomes a scoutmaster and teaches kids how to talk squirrel talk. Pacha gets to keep his home on the hill. It is a Disney ending for sure.

10. The Hunchback of Notre Dame

Walt Disney Pictures (1996)

Producers: Roy Conli, Don Hahn

Associate Producer: Philip Lofaro

Directors: Gary Trousdale, Kirk Wise

Writing Credits: Victor Hugo (novel *Notre-Dame de Paris*), Irene Mecchi, Tab Murphy (story), Jonathan Roberts, Bob Tzudiker, Noni White

Film Editor: Ellen Keneshea

Art Director: David Goetz

Animators: James Bake (rough inbetween artist Djali), James Baxter (supervising animator Quasimodo), Noreen Beasley (rough inbetweener), Saul Andrew Blinkoff (breakdown animator Hugo), David Brewster (animator), Dave Burgess (supervising animator Archdeacon), Jay N. Davis (assistant animator), Russ Edmonds (supervising animator Phoebus), Will Finn (supervising animator Laverne), Tony Fucile (supervising animator Esmeralda), Raul Garcia (animator), Ed Ghertner (layout supervisor), Jean Gillmore (character designer), Brian Wesley Green (assistant animator), Kris Heller (assistant animator), Mark Henley (scene planner), T. Daniel

Hofstedt (animator "Gargoyles" unit), Ron Husband (supervising animator Djali), Mike "Moe" Merell (animator), Robb Pratt (rough inbetweener), David Pruiksma (supervising animator Victor and Hugo), Mark Pudleiner (character animator Esmeralda), Chris Sauve (animator), Lon Smart (breakdown artist Phoebus), Michael Surrey (supervising animator Clopin), Kathy Zielinski (supervising animator Frollo)

Voice Cast: Tom Hulce (Quasimodo), Demi Moore (Esmeralda), Tony Jay (Judge Claude Frollo), Kevin Kline (Captain Phoebus), Paul Kandel (Clopin), Jason Alexander (Hugo), Charles Kimbrough (Victor), Mary Wickes (Laverne), David Ogden Stiers (the Archdeacon), Heidi Mollenhauer (Esmeralda singing voice), Mary Kay Bergman (Quasimodo's mother), Corey Burton (Brutish Guard), Jim Cummings (Misc. Guards and Gypsies), Bill Fagerbakke (Oafish Guard), Patrick Pinney (Misc. Guards and Gypsies), Gary Trousdale (the Old Heretic), Frank Welker (Baby Bird), Jane Withers (Laverne, additional dialogue)

Overview

Victor Hugo's novel is one of the great and dark works of literature. It is clear from the bonus extras audio commentary that the Disney team struggled with this from the start. On one hand, they wanted to capture the spirit of the novel and, on the other, they didn't want to scare six-year-olds with sexual obsessions and such. The final result is a beautiful frustration of a movie in my view. Combining 2-D and 3-D, the studio delivered what is without a doubt one of the most gorgeous animated films I have ever seen. I only wish they had not worried so much about those six-year-olds in the audience and that they had trusted Victor Hugo a bit more.

This movie's villain, Frollo, reflects a certain kind of thinking about villains in animated movies. He is unrepentant, not very introspective, evil, and cruel to the point of being a monster. I contend that this kind of one-dimensional villain is not as frightening as one in which the audience gets to see the character's internal struggle. **A villain is a hero in his own life. Everybody acts to survive in the world, even if they are making bad choices.** A villain is ideally an identifiable regular person with a fatal flaw. Cruella de Vil's flaw was vanity, for example. Frollo's fundamentalist worldview is probably his flaw. He measures evil against an inflexible standard. I wish the director and animators had allowed us to see more of Frollo's torment. Given the premise on which they are building this character, however, the performance is excellent. In my analysis, I will comment on Frollo perhaps more than any other character, suggesting ways he might have gained more dimension without scaring the kids.

Analysis

Chapter 1: "The Bells of Notre Dame/Main Title"

I recommend that you adjust the setup on the DVD so that, for the first chapter only, there are English captions (for the hearing impaired) appearing under the images on screen. The reason is that the opening song, "The Bells of Notre Dame," contains an incredible amount of backstory. In the audio narration, the producer and directors explain that they tried various ways to introduce the characters of Frollo and Quasimodo, but they all seemed "flat." Their solution was to allow lyricist Steven Swartz to put it all in a song. There is so much backstory contained in this song, in fact, that you can easily miss some of it if you are listening to the song and watching the fast-moving images on screen. The subtitles help a lot.

A synopsis of what is contained in that song goes like this: Gypsies are trying to covertly sneak into Paris at night. Judge Claude Frollo, a man who has longed to purge the world of vice and sin, sets a trap for them. The Gypsy mother flees with her baby, and Frollo chases her on horseback. She seeks refuge at the cathedral of Notre Dame. Frollo catches up to her, grabs the baby, and flings the mother onto the concrete steps, killing her. Without taking a second look at the woman on the ground, Frollo looks at the baby, decrees that it is "a demon monster" and tries to toss it down a nearby well. The cathedral's Archdeacon stops him, accusing Frollo of having spilled innocent blood on the church steps. He tells Frollo that he may hide his guilt from himself and his minions, but he can never hide from "the eyes of Notre Dame." Frollo has a rush of fear for his immortal soul and asks what he can do to save himself. The Archdeacon tells him he must raise the baby as his own. Frollo wants no part of that, but agrees so long as the baby lives out of sight in the Notre Dame cathedral. Then Frollo names the baby Quasimodo, which means "half-formed." After that, we have a passage of time during which Quasimodo grows up to be a misshapen young man. We begin the movie twenty years after that fateful night by the well.

The use of atmosphere in this first chapter is marvelous. It doesn't get much better. Notice how the damp darkness of the canal affects the Gypsies as they move toward downtown Paris. The cobblestone streets of the city cause sound to reverberate in a different way, and the filmmakers took advantage of that, too. When Frollo chases the Gypsy mother through the streets, you can almost feel the chill.

The puppet show storytelling device works nicely, even if maybe they tried to convey too much information with it. I particularly like the part where Quasimodo ages twenty years.

Notice how he and a priest are conveyed up the cathedral stairs in silhouette? Look closely and you will see the supporting sticks of the puppet master. The acting of the puppet-Quasimodo, even in silhouette, is nice.

In terms of performance, the primary character who catches my attention in Chapter 1 is Frollo. He almost literally comes out of the chute kicking babies down the stairs. He wears black and rides a black horse and is every inch a stereotypical Disney villain. The thing is that villains do not think they are villains. If you intend for the audience to empathize with a character, you must give them something they can relate to. In this first chapter we learn that Frollo is a God-fearing moral fundamentalist who is capable of extreme cruelty.

Chapter 2: "Will Today Be the Day?"

We meet Quasimodo for the first time. He's sweet, lonely, misshapen, and talks to birds and gargoyles. He longs to join the revelers below the cathedral in their yearly Festival of Fools, but Frollo has forbidden him to leave the building.

It is easy to empathize with Quasimodo. We all can relate to feelings of loneliness. Remember, **emotion tends to lead to action. Quasimodo's sadness is what leads him to try to sneak out for a brief visit to Festival of Fools. If he had simply curled up in the corner and cried, we would be feeling more sympathy than empathy. This is a very important acting distinction.**

The gargoyles are a device that allows Quasimodo to talk to himself. He is the only one who thinks they live. As soon as Frollo enters, they again become immobile. Every storyteller has to deal with the problem of how to communicate inner thought process for a character alone on stage. The trick is to justify it. This team chose talking gargoyles.

One more thing: Notice the little figurines in Quasimodo's play area. There is a figurine of Quasimodo himself plus one of

Frollo. I suspect the figurines are part of a Disney marketing strategy with Burger King. For sure they are not in the original novel.

Chapter 3: "Frollo Arrives"

Note the status transaction when Frollo enters, looming so tall over Quasimodo. Frollo seems to become more erect in his posture, and Quasimodo seems to bend slightly forward, sending his power center into the floor.

Quasimodo's behavior as he prepared the table for lunch caused me to empathize. Even though Frollo is an awful human being, Quasimodo is happy to see him. The presence of any other human in the bell tower is probably a welcome event and, at any rate, children rarely find fault with their parents even if they are abusive. Quasimodo may be twenty years old chronologically, but he is a young boy in terms of maturity. Do you see how he scampers to place the dishes on the table? He doesn't drag his feet in a depressed way. Happiness is the emotion, and the emotion is leading to the physical action of scampering.

When Frollo reviews the alphabet with Quasimodo, note the hunchback's delight with correct answers. There is a negotiation going on here. Quasimodo's objective is to earn Frollo's approval. The obstacle is the difficulty of the quiz.

At the very end of the chapter, we learn that Frollo has lied to Quasimodo about how his mother died, painting himself as a savior rather than a murderer. If Frollo has any conflict with himself about this, it doesn't show.

Chapter 4: "Frollo's Warning About the World 'Out There'"

This is an interesting chapter. Why is Frollo so intent upon keeping Quasimodo inside the cathedral? It has been twenty years after all. The song he sings ("Out There") suggests that he is only concerned with Quasimodo's feelings. The world is cruel, he sings, and Quasimodo is ugly. Insensitive people will taunt him.

Frollo's use of gesture is powerful. **A gesture does not have to be merely an illustration of the spoken line.** (See *On the Technique of Acting* by Michael Chekhov, Harper Resource, 1991.) Notice how often he physically touches Quasimodo. He caresses his face, strokes his unruly hair lovingly. All the while he is doing this, he is manipulating and controlling him. It is almost as if Frollo is training a dog, first with reward and then with admonishment. The acting in this sequence is complex and quite good, I think.

Late in the chapter, Frollo takes the lead and returns to Quasimodo's living quarters. He crosses to the figurines and begins to use them to illustrate his point. At the end, he literally places the figurine of Quasimodo back into the bell tower of the pretend cathedral. **A rule of acting is that you must have a reason for exiting or entering a scene.** When Frollo leads Quasimodo back to his living quarters, he must have in mind using those figurines to cement his argument. This is clever filmmaking. They managed to motivate the move and once again hold those Burger King figurines up for display.

Chapter 5: "Quasimodo Longs to Be 'Out There'"

Quasimodo is obedient but not convinced. He longs to spend one day "out there" among the regular people in the world.

In terms of scene construction and characterization, Quasimodo mainly has conflict with his situation. When he swings from one precariously high vantage point on the cathedral to another, he is literally grappling with conflict. We in the audience empathize and smile because Quasimodo has dreams. He doesn't give up; he keeps trying to survive. If he curled up in bed and slept away the depression, we would not be so enamored with him. At the final crescendo moment of his song, note the birds that fly by in the foreground. This hearkens back to Chapter 2 when he released the young bird for his first flight. Birds are free. This is nice visual storytelling.

Chapter 6: "Phoebus' Return to Paris"

Note the transaction between Phoebus and the bully Captain when they draw weapons on one another. In the previous sequence, the Captain's power center was lower. He now sees that Phoebus is a lieutenant and outranks him, and he is immediately in a state of anxiety. As I have pointed out several times in this book, **anxiety is a high and heady power center. An anxious character will gesticulate more with the upper part of his body. In general, confidence manifests itself in a character as a lower power center.**

During the first meeting between Phoebus and Frollo, Frollo says, "My last Captain of the Guard was a bit of a disappointment to me," at which time we hear the snapping of a harsh whip in the background. Note that Frollo cracks a quick sadistic grin in response to that whipping sound. My opinion is that the grin was not necessary. In fact, the moment would have been more chilling if he had just ignored the sound because he is accustomed to it. I would rather have focused on Phoebus's reaction to the sound and the fact that Frollo is immune to it.

Replay the short sequence and note that Phoebus's reaction to the whip noise is a mere startle reflex. He looks in the wrong direction. That doesn't make sense. When he first entered the scene, he heard the whipping going on and knew very well where it was coming from. When he hears it again in this moment, it is logical that he would look directly toward the room where he heard it earlier.

Chapter 7: "The Festival of Fools" ("Topsy Turvy")

You might want to once again turn on—just for this chapter—the captions for the hearing impaired. As in the opening sequence, this one has a lot of information tied up in the lyrics of a song.

Quasimodo joins the crowds at the Festival of Fools and is crowned the King of Fools. The people cheer him because they think he is wearing an ugly mask. Quasimodo, being so good-natured, doesn't really get the joke.

The animation in this chapter is awesome. Performance does not need to be subtle because of the carnival atmosphere.

Chapter 8: "The Crowd Turns on Their King"

Quasimodo learns about the cruelty of a mob. There is a lot of wonderful animation in this short chapter but not much opportunity for subtle acting. At one point Frollo says to Phoebus that "a lesson needs to be learned." He has that sick sadistic look on his face again. It would probably have been more powerful if we had a slightly closer shot of Frollo at that moment and if his expression reflected the difficulty of administering tough love. It would have given us a little more insight into Frollo's mind and value system.

Chapter 9: "Esmeralda Comes to Quasimodo's Aid"

Most of this chapter is taken up with a beautiful and fun chase sequence. For performance, we mainly have the opening moments when Esmeralda confronts Frollo across the crowd and the later meeting between Frollo and a shamed Quasimodo.

Esmeralda and Frollo almost seem to be tossing thunderbolts at one another across the heads of the crowd. They come across as very equal human beings once Frollo is isolated.

The status transaction between Frollo and Quasimodo could not be any more powerful. Quasimodo is shamed absolutely. His power center is inches from the ground. He is forced to look up at a dramatic angle to make eye contact with Frollo, who is atop a horse. Very nice staging in the scene.

Story-wise, Phoebus is somewhat weakened in this chapter. **Remember, unless you have a purely transitional sequence, a character should 100 percent of the time be playing an action in pursuit of an objective while overcoming an obstacle. Obstacle is equivalent to conflict. There are only three kinds of conflict: with self, with the situation, and with another character.** When Frollo orders Phoebus to capture Esmeralda, he responds without hesitation and has no evident conflict about it. Yet in an earlier sequence, he already came to her rescue. He for sure knows who she is by this point. When Frollo gives the order to capture her, my sense of things is that Phoebus should falter, even if imperceptibly. Conflict with himself and conflict with the situation.

Chapter 10: "Esmeralda Seeks Refuge in the Cathedral"

The physical distance between people is a status transaction. You and I will negotiate how close we stand to one another when we converse. We usually do not like it when mere acquaintances move too closely into our personal space. We reserve that space for intimates and family. Note that when Phoebus and Esmeralda approach one another after their introductory sword fight, it looks as though they are about to kiss. Now, I am as romantic as the next person, but I thought that was too much closeness, too soon. I would have preferred that they keep more of a distance in that moment and that we see their feeling for one another in their facial reactions.

Phoebus's character development is still shallow in this chapter. When Frollo confronts the two of them in that near-kiss moment, Phoebus goes into something of a panic. He tells Esmeralda to ask for sanctuary. She refuses and so he pretends she said it anyway. It seems to me this moment would have worked better if Phoebus had immediately mentioned her having asked for sanctuary, and then for Phoebus and Esmeralda to exchange a knowing look that says, in effect, "I didn't ask for sanctuary and you know it." It is worrisome that Phoebus hasn't shown more character and strength. Esmeralda has to be romantically attracted to him, after all.

Chapter 11: "Frollo's Threat"

Disney movies have always approached human sexuality in an awkward fashion. This is why perhaps Victor Hugo's *Hunchback of Notre Dame* was not a good candidate for the Disney treatment in the first place. Frollo's sexually tormented nature is hinted at when he grasps Esmeralda from behind and buries his nose in her luxuriant and earthy hair. But the moment and the dialogue afterward is cryptic enough to keep young children in the dark about what the heck is going on. My opinion is that it would have been okay to be a little more overt without becoming graphic. Kids see more sexuality than that on after-school TV these days.

Chapter 12: "God Help the Outcasts"

We get to listen to a syrupy show tune, and the chapter doesn't have any acting that I can see. It is all designed to evoke mood. Very lovely building, beautifully lit with candles. Quasimodo comes downstairs to hear Esmeralda sing, but there is no conflict involved in that.

Chapter 13: "Esmeralda Follows Quasimodo into His World"

Some townspeople appear in the cathedral, yelling at Quasimodo: "You! Bell ringer! What are you doing down here? Haven't you caused enough trouble already?" I do not think it was necessary to bring those characters in at this point. It would have been stronger to have Esmeralda look up from her reverie, see Quasimodo leaning against the pillar, and then try to approach him. Quasimodo, suddenly in conflict with his situation for being away from the bell tower, would then run back upstairs, and she would follow. It looks to me like the reason for having the townspeople arrive was simply to propel Quasimodo back upstairs. It works, but the same objective could have been accomplished in a more character-revealing way and with less animation.

Once Esmeralda is in Quasimodo's living quarters, the action moves directly to those figurines again. Now we learn that, in fact, Quasimodo carves the figurines himself. There is a great sculptor (or maybe even an animator!) beneath that misshapen body!

There is a minor negotiation when Quasimodo argues that Esmeralda should view the city sunset and he tries to convince her that she can remain in the cathedral forever.

This chapter feels a lot like a first date. The characters are very responsive to one another. **Acting is reacting. The performances in Quasimodo's living quarters are strong in that regard. Each of them seems to be listening to the other, which is a key.** Stage actors learn that one of the hardest things to do is to actually listen to what another actor is saying without thinking about what your next line is.

Chapter 14: "Quasimodo Helps Esmeralda Escape"

This is an action sequence. Not a lot of acting going on.

Chapter 15: "Phoebus Comes Looking for Esmeralda"

Emotion tends to lead to action. The extreme degree of Quasimodo's attack on Phoebus reflects the depth of his anger. He is beyond angry, it seems, and is close to fury. The personality conversion is dramatic and is also a foreshadowing of the power Quasimodo will display later in the story.

Chapter 16: "Quasimodo Dreams of 'Heaven's Light'"

Quasimodo is lonely and in love. From an acting perspective, the most telling moment is at the end when he rings the bells with a new purpose. The emotion is elevated and so is his physical response to it.

Chapter 17: "Hell Fire"

We finally get a glimpse into Frollo's heart. He is in terrible conflict with himself and with his situation. His fundamentalist religious views leave no room for weaknesses of the flesh or compromise. He cannot resolve his lustful feelings and so he blames them on the devil. Esmeralda, in his mind, is an agent of evil. He frames only two possible solutions to the conflict: (1) Esmeralda will repent and reject the devil, falling into Frollo's bed or (2) Frollo will kill her. Note the tension in Frollo's body and the way he flails toward heaven. His movements are motivated by overpowering emotion and conflict. This is an excellent sequence and high drama.

After the Hell Fire musical sequence, Frollo begins his obsessive search for Esmeralda. He considers the Gypsies to be human vermin and does not hesitate to torment them.

Phoebus continues to be a frustratingly bland character from an acting perspective. He rarely appears to be playing an action in pursuit of an objective. In this chapter, he simply shakes his head disapprovingly when he sees Frollo mistreating the Gypsies. I think it would be stronger if he were under increasing conflict about his role as Frollo's Captain of the Guard versus his role as a human being. We are getting a slight hint of the conflict, but not nearly enough.

Chapter 18: "Phoebus Defies Frollo"

Note the sequence in which Frollo passes the torch to Phoebus. Phoebus accepts it and then backs away. He hesitates, evidently in conflict with himself about whether to burn the building or not—and then he plunges the torch into the water bucket. It suggests that the exchange would have been more powerful if Phoebus has resisted accepting the torch in the first place. Let Frollo hold it out toward Phoebus, waiting for him to take it. Then we would have a cleaner conflict between characters. Phoebus and Frollo could glare at each other, and then Phoebus could grab the torch and immediately extinguish it.

Chapter 19: "One of a Kind (A Guy Like You)"

This is a show tune sequence that could probably have been left out of the movie with no damage done. It does not advance the plot, exposes no new character information, and it involves no acting. On the positive side, the song is cute, and it provides an opportunity for the gargoyles to clown around.

Chapter 20: "The Fugitive ('Heaven's Light' Reprise)"

The sequence in which Esmeralda kisses Phoebus is worth examining. First, look at the exchange between the new lovers. **A scene**

is a negotiation, and each character should be playing an action.
What we have right now is a fairly generic lover's clinch. The scene
could have evoked more power if, after Phoebus says that maybe
the arrow punctured his heart, he had looked into her eyes, maybe
tried to kiss her—and *then* passed out. She could have kissed him
anyway, but it would have had more voltage. It would have been
something like a kiss of life. After the kiss, he could stir slightly so
that we know he is not dead. That way, Phoebus's imminent death
becomes Esmeralda's obstacle. The scene would still have the same
impact on Quasimodo, who is watching from the shadows, but it
would arguably have had a stronger theatrical construction. It is
always useful to think of a scene as a negotiation.

Quasimodo reacts to all of this first with disbelief, then
shock, and then grief. The animators successfully put him
through all of those changes, but I think there is maybe too
much physical movement. In the bonus extras audio narration,
the directors joke about making certain that the six-year-olds in
the audience would know that Quasimodo's heart is breaking.
This is one of those places where I think Western animators
could take a clue from Miyazaki. He would have handled the
reaction with more stillness, and I think that would be more
emotionally satisfying. Right now, Quasimodo is hanging onto
that wooden beam, turning his back to the action, squirming
around, and then turning back again. Tears tumble freely down
his cheeks, and he tears up the ace of spades. It seems to me that
the audience knows what the stakes are for Quasimodo by this
point. A six-year-old might not conceptually understand affairs
of the heart, but he has probably seen his parents kissing. I think
I would have liked the sequence more if Quasimodo forced himself to watch what he did not want to see. Forcing himself to
watch would become his action. The obstacle would be his pain.
Tears might well up in his eyes and, as they started to fall down
his cheek, they too would become an obstacle, and he would

lower his head to hide them from Esmeralda—protecting his dignity. **The truth is that, in real life, we humans do not easily share our emotions with one another.**

Chapter 21: "Another Visit from Frollo"

The acting in the Frollo/Quasimodo lunch table sequence is good. I like the way the characters are listening to one another, and I like the way Quasimodo is trying to hide his fear. Emotion tends to lead to action. The emotion is fear, and the thing it leads to is trying to hide it.

Frollo is by now so obsessed that he is out of his mind. He is utterly irrational and furious. We see that by the force with which he destroys the table display and then burns the figurine of Esmeralda. All of that is way-over-the-top acting, and the only way to justify it is for him to be near crazy. I wish the storytellers had made other choices regarding Frollo. Here in Chapter 21, it would be nice if we could gain a little more insight into his personal struggle as a man. It is hard to empathize with madness, and they are putting him too much on that side of the equation. Given the choices they made, however, they presented it well. The scene construction works well, and there are clear negotiations.

Note the sequence in which Phoebus asks Quasimodo if he is coming with him to find Esmeralda. Quasimodo says he can't, and when Phoebus presses, he says, "Frollo is my master. I can't disobey him again." At that point, he wraps his arms around himself and turns his back on Phoebus. Stage actors learn to be careful about that kind of move. **You want to always make acting choices that invite the most conflict. When you make an acting choice that says, in essence, "I don't want to talk to you" or "I do not want to be in this scene any more," you are moving away from conflict.** This sequence would have had more punch to it if

Quasimodo had not turned his back. He could have faced Phoebus defiantly and then maybe dropped his gaze in shame, which would have triggered the same response in Phoebus.

Chapter 22: "The Court of Miracles"

Mostly, this chapter is a long series of action sequences. They are interspersed with small moments that involve acting, like when Esmeralda interrupts the hanging and when Frollo arrives. My only note is that, given Frollo's mental state in the previous chapter, I would like to see him struggling harder to maintain mental control now. The way it is presented, he is sort of back to his controlled awful self. In order to make him more interesting, there needs to be more conflict. And the most opportunity for conflict is with himself. His confrontation with Esmeralda, Phoebus, and Quasimodo is not really a negotiation because there is no way they can win.

Chapter 23: "A Public Execution"

When Frollo offers Esmeralda the bargain of life, I wish so much that we had been able to see some of his need in addition to his madness. **It is a useful acting exercise to ask yourself what your character needs in a scene. Try converting "want" to "need" and see what you get.** The way the sequence is presented, he is still smirking and snarling and is still being drawn in consistently dark colors. The man is in pain! Pain involves struggle. Struggle is part of life on earth. As awful a person as Frollo is, he is still a human. I want to understand what makes him tick. Perhaps a couple of muscle twitches in his face during close-up would have helped. Perhaps if the crowd was screaming for him to burn her. There are various ways he could have been made to display more emotion in the moment. In the audio narration, the directors mention that there was a deleted scene that took place the night before the execution, in the dungeon. This scene also appears in Victor Hugo's novel. In it, Frollo declares his love for Esmeralda. The directors say they decided against using it for "expediency" and because it was too dark.

Quasimodo, meanwhile, seems to have given up and gone into depression. That is understandable perhaps, but it is a weak acting choice. A character needs to be doing something 100 percent of the time, and falling into depression does not qualify. I would have liked it more if he was unsuccessfully tugging at his chains, trying to free himself. The gargoyles could urge him on and, after a moment of collapse, he could lunge successfully, breaking the chains.

Chapter 24: "Quasimodo Rescues Esmeralda"

Another action sequence. Beautiful animation, not a lot of acting.

Chapter 25: "Frollo Attacks Notre Dame"

Another action sequence. Beautiful animation, still not a lot of acting.

Chapter 26: "A Short-Lived Moment of Triumph"

This is a very nice scene. The acting is truthful and subtle. I particularly like that Quasimodo tries to give her that spoonful of water. We act to survive. If he had gone from "Oh, no!" to a collapse in tears, it would not have been as powerful a moment. The water gives him something to *do*, making conflict in the scene.

Chapter 27: "Unfinished Business"

Frollo attempts to murder Quasimodo. There is no hesitation or second thought, just raw evil. There is no understanding the man. He is a nutcase. Given that premise, the scene works just fine. I personally wish it were not quite so easy for Frollo to run a knife into Quasimodo's hump.

Chapter 28: "The Final Confrontation"

Big action sequence. Even in death, Frollo has no regrets. He is only sorry that he is dying. In the end, however, what have we really learned? Bad men do bad things? There is good and there is evil in the world? Could it possibly be that there lurks the potential for evil in all of us, as well as the potential for good? Would that not have made a more valuable point?

Chapter 29: "Sweet Reunion"

There is not much complexity to the performances in this final chapter. Everybody is happy. Hugs all around. Quasimodo never again has to live in the bell tower.

11. The Road to El Dorado

DreamWorks SKG (2000)

Executive Producers: Jeffrey Katzenberg, Bill Damaschke

Coproducers: Brooke Breton, Bonne Radford

Directors: Bibo Bergeron, Will Finn, Don Paul, David Silverman, Jeffrey Katzenberg

Writers: Ted Elliott, Edmund Fong (story), Henry Mayo, Terry Rossio

Film Editors: John Carnochan, Vicki Hiatt, Dan Molina

Art Directors: Paul Lasaine, Wendell Luebbe, Raymond Zibach

Animators: James Baxter (senior supervising animator), David Bowers (story artist), David Brewster (supervising animator), Ricardo Curtis (animator), Rick Farmiloe (animator), Lionel Gallat (animator), Maximilian Graenitz (senior animator), Rodolphe Guenoden (supervising animator Chel), Rene Harnois Jr. (3-D character coordinator), Todd Jacobsen (key assistant animator Chel), Jakob Hjort Jensen (character animator), Marek Kochout (animator), Ted Mathot (story artist), Simon Otto (animator), Jane Poole (animator Chel), Brian Riley (scene planner), Erik Chr. Schmidt (character animator supervising all miscellaneous 2-D and 3-D characters), Amy Taylor (animation coordinator), Dimos Vrysellas (character animator Miguel), Greg Whittaker (animator Stone Jaguar), Alexander Williams (animator), James C. J. Williams (scene planning supervisor)

Voice Cast: Kevin Kline (Tulio), Kenneth Branagh (Miguel), Rosie Perez (Chel), Armand Assante (Tzekel-Kan), Edward James Olmos (Chief), Jim Cummings (Cortes/Others), Frank Welker (Altivo/Others), Tobin Bell (Zaragoza), Duncan Marjoribanks (Acolyte), Elijah Chiang (Kid #1), Cyrus Shaki-Khan (Kid #2), Elton John (Narrator)

Overview

The Road to El Dorado seems to have been loosely inspired by the old Bing Crosby and Bob Hope road movies. There were many of them. That's not a bad idea on the surface, but Bing and Bob had innate charm and were big stars of their day. The success of those road movies was largely a factor of star persona.

The two main characters in *The Road to El Dorado,* by contrast, are not known to us and so we have to discover their values via the unfolding of this story. In my view, that is a problem for the storytellers because they are beginning with characters that are immature, opportunistic, small-time crooks.

Analysis

Chapter 1: "El Dorado (Main Titles)"

We are introduced first to the time and place of our story, Spain 1519, and then to the two leading characters, Tulio (Kevin Kline) and Miguel (Kenneth Branagh). The first time we see their images is on a "wanted" poster. The reward? One hundred doublons. The images come to life and we discover Miguel and Tulio cheating at craps. In terms of scene construction, each of them would be in pursuit of the same objective, namely collecting a bunch of money. The obstacle/conflict is with their situation. If they are caught cheating, they'll be beaten or killed. In the sequence, they go from action to action, horsing around, clowning for the group of rogues, tossing dice, always in pursuit of the money.

Chapter 2: "Loaded Dice"

Play an action until something happens to make you play a different action. Once it is discovered that they have been playing with loaded dice, the objective changes. Now they want to escape, and they have conflict with their situation as well as with the other characters.

The bow from the rooftop is pure vaudeville. Shades of Bob Hope and Bing Crosby, and it works.

The entire chapter is a long action sequence without any opportunity for subtle acting.

Chapter 3: "Stowaways"

Let's talk for a moment about Altivo the white horse and his relationship to human characters in the movie. The storytellers have made Altivo as smart as—and sometimes smarter than—the human characters in head-to-head transactions. That breaks Shakespeare's dictum that actors should hold the mirror up to nature. Horses may be very smart in the hierarchy of animals, but they are not smarter than humans. Tulio tries to bribe Altivo with a red apple into fetching a pry-bar and, instead, the horse brings a full set of jail keys. This strains credibility for horse behavior, even in animation. The writers must have sensed that something was wrong with this because they had Miguel remind Tulio that he is "talking to a dumb horse." Instead of treating the horse like a horse, they made a gag out of it. I think this gag comes at too high a price in terms of character credibility.

In a movies like *The Lion King, Finding Nemo, Antz,* and *A Bug's Life,* the animals/insects are human-level smart and it works because they exist in an animal world. In the DreamWorks movie *Spirit: Stallion of the Cimarron,* the lead-character horse was often smarter than the humans, and I didn't think it worked there either. In old TV shows like *Rin Tin Tin* and *Lassie,* the dogs were super-smart and pushed the envelope of conceptual cleverness, but at the end of the day they were still dogs and slept in the doghouse.

The main action in this chapter is to establish that Cortez is a real person, and we are likely to meet him again.

Chapter 4: "Overboard"

After Tulio, Miguel, and the horse are in the rowboat, there is little negotiation in scenes. Mainly, action sequences. Beautiful animation and superb visual effects, though.

Chapter 5: "Beached"

The opening sequence, in which the boys reflect on their lives, lacks tension. A character should be playing an action 100 percent of the time, and neither of them is at the beginning of the chapter. Yes, they are trying to stay alive, and, yes, the conflict is the fact that they are in a rowboat at sea, but basically they have given up rowing or bailing water or trying to survive in any way. They are victims to the waves.

When they find sand in their hands, the action shifts. The acting is quite strong in their reactions to the sand. Play the sequence frame by frame, and you will see that Tulio reacts in a different way than does Miguel. Very nice.

Emotion tends to lead to action. Their happiness is powerful, and so they kiss the ground. They do not simply get out of the boat and jump up and down. They kiss the ground. **The more powerful the emotion, the more you can justify in terms of**

extreme action. For a reference, check out Charlie Chaplin in *Gold Rush.* Look at the sequence where he celebrates the fact that Virginia, the dance-hall girl, has accepted the dinner invitation.

Play an action until something happens to make you play a different action. As they are kissing the ground, they encounter the bones and skull. Big reaction. Happiness changes to fear. Fear motivates the retreat to the boat. Then Tulio notices that the map fits the island they are on. Now we have yet another change. **The important thing from a performance perspective is that your characters go from action to action to action. It needs to be seamless.** The acting in this beach sequence is quite good.

Chapter 6: "The Trail We Blaze"

This chapter is an opportunity to play an Elton John song. There is not much going on in terms of performance.

Chapter 7: "Great Big Rock"

There is not much opportunity for subtle performance in this chapter, but the action moves forward in a logical fashion. There is continual conflict either between characters or between a character and his situation. There are shifting objectives and actions, and it all fits together in a seamless fashion.

Chapter 8: "Entering El Dorado"

Acting is reacting, and Tulio and Miguel react to the beautiful gold city. The backgrounds in this chapter are awesomely beautiful.

Chapter 9: "Stopping the Volcano"

This chapter has several object lessons to talk about. First, notice Miguel's reaction after Tzekel-Kan cries out, "Citizens! Did I not predict that the gods would come to us?" He looks behind him, then at Tulio, and then catches on that maybe he and Tulio are thought to be gods. He murmurs slyly, "Hmmmmmm. . . ." I think that reaction is not quite right given the context. Neither of them should yet catch on. Mentally, Miguel's thought process should still be trying to sort things out. An expression of affable confusion would make more sense. (If you want to read more about the importance of sequential thought, check out another book I wrote, *The Actor's Field Guide: Acting Notes on the Run,* Backstage Books, 2004, p. 91.)

As Chief Tannabok introduces himself, Tzekel-Kan frowns. I think that is too obvious a giveaway about their relationship. I would have preferred to have Tzekel-Kan maintain his fake charm. We will find out soon enough that these two men are competitors.

When Miguel dismounts, he catches his foot in Altivo's harness. That is a very good Charlie Chaplin gag. **Remember, drama has to do with man's potential; comedy has to do with his limitations.** Miguel may be getting the idea that the natives consider him to be important, but he is still not so important that he can't snag his foot in a harness. The gag brings him down from his momentary self-inflation. I only wish there had been one more bit in which he tries to untangle his foot. That would have been *really* Charlie Chaplin!

Altivo the horse should not have climbed the steep steps to the temple. This is more unhorselike behavior. I have serious doubts about a horse being able to navigate that many small and vertical steps. Anyway, how is the horse going to get back down?

Chapter 10: "Cheldorado"

As the boys are celebrating their con, Altivo sees the girl and tries to warn Tulio and Miguel of her presence. Again, this is not credible behavior for the horse.

Chel wants in on the scam. She actually uses that very word: "scam." My first thought is, "Where did she learn a word like that?

She's a native, isn't she? *Scam* is a twentieth-century word, isn't it?" This, of course, is not an animator's problem. That is what somebody wrote and what Rosie Perez recorded. I compiled the following descriptions of Chel from the bonus extras audio narration. Taken together, they are very revealing, because they explain almost nothing about the character. Take a look: Chel is "a street-savvy native," "a barrel of laughs . . . she loves life and yet she's frustrated by life," "very sassy and opinionated," "she's tough and sensitive," "shy but extremely forward," and "She's every bit as clever and manipulative and smart and devious as they are." As a character analysis, none of this is particularly helpful. Most of the described traits simply cancel one another out. What we want to know is how she got to be like that. Are her parents around? What is she so angry about? Does she have siblings? What are her dreams? What makes her laugh? Is she religious? Is she a virgin?

Chapter 11: "It's Tough to Be a God"

We get a colorful and musical glimpse into the daily routine of Tulio, Miguel, and Altivo the horse. There isn't much acting in this chapter.

Chapter 12: "A Proper Tribute"

The acting in the human sacrifice sequence is top notch. The poor sap comes within an inch of death, and when Miguel grasps him under his arms, he faints dead away. I'm so glad they didn't play that moment for a gag.

The Chief offers gold as a tribute to the gods, asking, "My lords, does this please you?" At that point Tulio swoons. I think the swoon was not necessary. It would have been a more honest acting moment if Tulio and Miguel had exchanged a quick glance and then acknowledged that this gold tribute would do.

This kind of over-the-top acting moment seems to be a sort of signature style of *The Road to El Dorado* by now. Maybe it hearkens back to the idea of vaudevillians on the road in a grand adventure. Bob Hope and Bing Crosby were often over the top and corny in their road movies.

Chapter 13: "Three Days"

Tulio and Miguel negotiate with the Chief for a boat. **A scene is a negotiation. In any negotiation, there must be a way to win and a way to lose.** If they get the boat, they win; if they do not, they lose. The conflict is with the situation more than with the Chief because the Chief wants to please them. Their situation is that they are bluffing and can still be killed if they are found out.

The next negotiation is between Tulio and Miguel (conflict with another character) over the conditions of "lying low" for three days. That negotiation is resolved when Miguel agrees to stay put.

Tulio then says to Chel, "Excuse me, I want to gloat over my gold." That is a weak transition for Tulio because gloating over his gold does not involve a negotiation. Ideally, he would be moving from action to action in a seamless way. The reason the storytellers did that, however, was to physically move Tulio aside so the action can shift to Chel. She has an objective of her own when she moves toward Miguel. She has conflict with the situation, and we are not certain at first what her objective is. **It is not necessary for the audience to know what a character's objective is. It is only necessary for her to have one.** As soon as she dispenses with Miguel, it becomes apparent that her objective was to be alone with Tulio.

When Tulio discovers that Miguel is gone, he tosses his hands in the air and starts moaning, "What am I going to do?" A stronger acting choice would have been to have him immediately chase after Miguel. Chel would stop him and we would still have the ensuing seduction sequence. Again, the idea is to go from action to action to action. This is twice in one chapter that Tulio has been caught with no theatrical action.

Tulio is sexually attracted to Chel, and Chel is doing most of the seducing. He has conflict with himself. He knows he ought not fool around with her, but he wants to anyway. The essence of conflict with self is "yes I will, no I won't, yes I will, no I won't." He gives in to his urges in the end, thereby losing the negotiation with himself. It would seem that if he gets the girl, he wins, but in this case, he is telling himself to leave her alone. He gives in and so he loses.

Chapter 14: "Age of the Jaguar"

This is my favorite Miguel sequence in the movie so far. For starters, we see that he loves beauty and appreciates nature. Observe his reaction to the birds flying by. Then we learn that, though he may be a rogue and adventurer, he has empathy for the underdog. He saves the native from being beaten. Then he picks up an instrument and begins to pluck its strings as playful children gather.

Chapter 15: "Without Question"

Miguel falls in love with the people of El Dorado. He is considering staying here forever. There are no scenes in this chapter and no negotiations of any significance. It is an opportunity to hear another cut from the Elton John CD.

Chapter 16: "Tzekel-Kan's Advice"

The opening negotiation in this chapter is funny. Tulio is amorously involved with Chel when Tzekel-Kan interrupts things. The action is to get himself together. The obstacle is that he is turned on. The objective is to fool Tzekel-Kan.

The sequence in which Tzekel-Kan negotiates for blood sacrifice is not really a negotiation. Tulio does not speak against blood sacrifice. From Tulio's perspective, the conflict is with his situation; from Tzekel-Kan's perspective, the conflict is with another person, namely Tulio. Tzekel-Kan thinks he wins his negotiation. Tulio doesn't win anything except a bit more time.

Tulio departs the temple to go find Miguel. That is a good transition. **Action leads to action.**

Chapter 17: "Play Ball"

Although it is all intended to be good fun, I very much wish Miguel and Tulio had found some other way than cheating to win the game. I regret the message this sends to the intended audience for *The Road to El Dorado*.

The animation in this chapter is wonderful. It is comprised of one long negotiation in which the boys try to win the game (action) so that they can survive (objective). The obstacle is that they are not gods and the opposing team would put the Green Bay Packers to shame.

Chapter 18: "No Sacrifices"

The acting in this chapter is strong and subtle. Tzekel-Kan goes through several changes: (1) delight at the prospect of having some sacrifices, (2) confusion when Miguel says he doesn't want any sacrifices, and (3) realization that Miguel is not a god after all because he bleeds. On his side of the transaction, Miguel admirably shows no hesitation in taking on Tzekel-Kan. He physically strikes the man and then kicks him out of El Dorado. I could argue that maybe Miguel should have exhibited just a tiny bit of doubt about his bravado paying off, but it is not a big deal. The scene works. It is a big negotiation.

Chapter 19: "Gods Don't Bleed"

Did you ever see the excellent 1975 live-action Sean Connery and Michael Caine movie *The Man Who Would Be King*? The payoff for that one was similar to this. One of the "gods" in that movie was discovered to be mortal because he bled.

The sequence on the boat, when Miguel tells the Chief it is a "complete do-over," is interesting from a performance perspective. Miguel is in conflict with himself ("I must leave; I don't want to leave") and with his situation ("This is another fine mess I've gotten myself into"). His action is to buy some more time in which to make up his mind about things. The Chief wants only to please the gods, so his negotiation is with the situation. If the gods want a complete do-over, then that is what we shall have. Then comes the transition in which the Chief apparently realizes that Miguel is a human, not a god. Rather than being threatened by this, the revelation seems to be a relief. He speaks to Miguel almost in a fatherly fashion, telling him he can stay forever in El Dorado if he wishes.

I like the Chief's final expression before he turns away, after "To err is human." The acting choice is strong there, letting us in the audience know that the Chief is playing along and is a total good guy.

Chapter 20: "Tulio and Chel—Deal?"

The negotiation between Tulio and Chel works okay, ending in a clinch. The problem character in the transaction is Miguel, who we discover loitering in the corner so that he can conveniently overhear Tulio's evident betrayal. It would have played more strongly if we had seen Miguel arrive. Action leads to action. In fact, I would have liked to see most of the Tulio vs. Chel negotiation from Miguel's POV. That would also have allowed us to see Tulio and Chel seal their deal by descending into the plush pillows for some more lovemaking.

The horse's reaction to Tulio and Chel is not right. It's too human. But if we are going to play the horse/human game, it would probably have been stronger to have the horse be initially charmed by the lovers, on the mistaken premise that Miguel is also charmed. Then Miguel could have popped him in the mouth or something. It would have been a transitional moment for the horse. But for my money, I'd have left Altivo out of the scene altogether. He doesn't add anything.

Chapter 21: "Jaguar Attacks"

We get open conflict/negotiation between Miguel and Tulio over the issue of whether to go or stay. Miguel's snide comment about Chel suggests there may be a twinge of jealousy involved here, too.

The jaguar sequences are wonderful action stuff. There isn't a lot of acting going on. The boys are trying to save their lives.

I wish Chel had taken the initiative to get on Altivo. As presented, the horse responds to the command, "Get Chel out of here!" A horse would not understand that kind of instruction, but Chel would.

Chapter 22: "Tzekel-Kan Emerges"

Note the status transaction between Tzekel-Kan and Cortes. Tzekel-Kan is convinced that this god is for real and he grovels, tossing his power center into the ground.

There is a nice acting moment between Tulio and Miguel as they are hanging from the vines. **Acting has almost nothing to do with words.** They look at one another and, without saying anything further, agree to go their separate ways. The animators expertly captured the thought sequence.

Chapter 23: "Friends Never Say Good-bye"

This is the most successful of the musical sequences because, underneath the song, there are miscellaneous nonverbal negotiations between the major characters. If you removed the music, the action would still play well, I think. Action to action, seamlessly, and continual negotiation. Each character seems to have an objective. The horse is acting relatively horselike.

Chapter 24: "Cortes Approaches"

The transitional moment is when everybody realizes that Cortes is approaching, led by Tzekel-Kan. Emotion tends to lead to action. The action shifts to Tulio, who will try to devise a plan for saving El Dorado.

Chapter 25: "Got a Wave to Catch"

Miguel's conversion back into a rogue opportunist does not satisfy emotionally. When did the conversion happen? When he was in midair on the horse? After he landed on the boat? I really wish we had been allowed to see that transition because it has major plot implications. What happened to all of that love for the El Dorado children back in Chapter 15? The storytellers buried it in a lot of exciting action animation. I would say that a 180-degree philosophic conversion of a major character ought to be shown on screen.

At the end of the chapter, with a boatload of gold plunder at stake, Tulio, Miguel, and Chel make the decision that their lives are worth more than the gold. The boat is rammed broadside into the wall of the waterfall, and the kids (and the horse) burst into freedom.

This visually exciting sequence is emotionally barren, unfortunately. The three characters we have spent this time with are still shallow, self-serving opportunists. They have expressed no remorse at all for being thieves.

Chapter 26: "There's No El Dorado Here"

We tie up the dangling plot line that involves Cortes and Tzekel-Kan. Tulio and Miguel formally make up and become partners in adventure and presumably partners in crime once again. Friendship is the highest virtue.

In the final analysis, the message behind this movie seems to be that situational ethics are okay.

12. Tarzan

Walt Disney Pictures (1999)

Producer: Bonnie Arnold

Associate Producer: Christopher Chase

Directors: Chris Buck, Kevin Lima

Film Editor: Gregory Perler

Art Director: Dan St. Pierre

Writing Credits: Edgar Rice Burroughs (novel *Tarzan of the Apes*), Tab Murphy, Bob Tzudiker, Noni White, Henry Mayo, David Reynolds, Jeffrey Stepakoff, Ned Teitelbaum

Animators: Georges Abolin (animator Tarzan), Pierre Alary (animator Tarzan), Marco Allard (animator Tarzan), James Baker (animator Clayton), Noreen Beasley (rough inbetweener Jane), Jared Beckstrand (animator Jane), Doug Bennett (animator Jane), Marco Berthier (animator Tarzan), Saul Andrew Blinkoff (assistant breakdown animator Terk), David Block (animator Porter), Bolhem Bouchiba (animator Tarzan), Robert Bryan (animator Jane), Robert Cardone (layout artist), Borja Montoro Cavero (animator Tarzan), Caroline Cruikshank (animator Jane), Patrick Delage (animator Tarzan), Eric Delbecq (animator Tarzan), Adam Dykstra (animator Terk), Russ Edmonds (supervising animator Kala), Marc Eoche-Duval (animator Sabor), Danny Galieote (animator Terk), Raul Garcia (animator), Tim George (animator Clayton), Jean Gillmore (character designer), Steven Pierre Gordon (animator Young and Baby Tarzan),

Thierry Goulard (animator Tarzan), Juanjo Guarnido (animator Sabor), Kris Heller (assistant animator Ape Family), Kent Holaday (assistant animator baboons and miscellaneous characters), Richard Hoppe (animator Clayton), James Hull (animator Tantor), Jay Jackson (supervising animator Gorilla Family), Jeff Johnson (animator Young and Baby Tarzan), Mark Koetsier (animator Jane), Doug Krohn (animator Jane), Mike Kunkel (animator), Zoltan Maros (animator Sabor), Mario J. Menjivar (animator Kala), Jean Morel (animator Tantor), David Nethery (additional clean-up animator), Joe Oh (character animator) Dorothea Baker Paul (clean-up artist Clayton), David Moses Pimentel (animator Terk), Jean Christophe Poulain (layout supervisor), Robb Pratt (animator Kerchak), Mark Pudleiner (additional animator), Stéphane Sainte-Foi (animator Tarzan), Lon Smart (key assistant animator Terk), Marc Smith (animator Kerchack), Chad Stewart (animator Terk), Michael Stocker (animator Clayton), George D. Sukara (clean-up animator), Yoshimichi Tamura (animator Young and Baby Tarzan), JC Tran-Quang-Thieu (animator Tarzan), Kristoff Vergne (animator Tarzan), Stevan Wahl (animator Tantor), Andreas Wessel-Therhorn (animator Kala), Dougg William (animator Kala), Theresa Wiseman (animator Porter), Enis Tahsin Özgür (animator Tarzan), Glen Keane (supervising animator Tarzan), Ken Duncan (supervising animator Jane), Randy Haycock (supervising animator Clayton), T. Daniel Hofstedt (supervising animator Captain and Thugs), Jay Jackson (supervising animator Gorilla Family), Dominique Monfery (supervising animator Sabor), John Ripa (supervising animator Young and Baby Tarzan), Sergio Pablos (supervising animator Tantor), Bruce W. Smith (supervising animator Kerchak), Michael Surrey (supervising animator Terk), Chris Wahl (supervising animator Flynt and Mungo), Dave Burgess (supervising animator Porter), Russ Edmonds (supervising animator Kala)

Voice Cast: Tony Goldwyn (Tarzan), Minnie Driver (Jane Porter), Glenn Close (Kala), Brian Blessed (Clayton), Nigel Hawthorne (Porter), Lance Henriksen (Kerchak), Wayne Knight (Tantor), Alex D. Linz (Young Tarzan), Rosie O'Donnell (Terk), Taylor Dempsey (Young Tantor), Jason Marsden (additional voices)

Overview

A key moment in the Disney version of *Tarzan* happens in Chapter 11 when Tarzan puts his hand up against Kala's and realizes he is "different" from his mother. To me, that gesture encapsulates the entire message of the movie. Especially today at the beginning of the twenty-first century, it is time to deal with the reality that the world is comprised of many dynamic and "different" tribes, and we had better all learn how to get along.

Another of Disney's movies, *The Hunchback of Notre Dame,* arguably suffered from the Disney warm-and-fuzzies. That one retained neither the edge nor the darkness of the famous novel on which it was based. But this *Tarzan* took the literacy source material and transformed it into something that, while not exactly the same as the book, is just as good, and maybe better. The movie is not so much about hunting for cities of gold as it is about hunting for where one belongs in the world. It is exploration of basic human values.

Analysis

Chapter 1: "Main Title/Two Worlds"

Prologue and backstory. Right away, it is clear that the performances in this movie are going to be strong. Notice how emotion is driving the action of Tarzan's family in the little boat;

meanwhile, Kala and Kerchak behave lovingly with their new baby. Take a specific look at Kala's facial expression the moment she realizes that Sabor the tiger is killing her baby. This is a surprisingly horrific moment for American animation in general and Disney animation in particular. Her reaction is actually to the terrified receding cries of her baby as the tiger drags it off into the jungle. There is a lot of heart in it.

Chapter 2: "Kala's Discovery"

The use of atmosphere in this chapter is excellent. Kala has never been inside a human home before, and this one smells of violence. Her animal instincts are alert at the same time as her more analytical self. Kala is very humanized, which makes it easy for us to empathize with her emotions. Her eyes are particularly expressive. The eyes are the window to the soul, as they say.

Notice how she recoils with her entire body when she finds the bloody bodies of Tarzan's parents. Fear is the emotion and recoiling is what she does about it. **Emotion tends to lead to action.**

Kala reaches to uncover the baby, has a brief second thought about it, and then goes ahead. That slight hesitation reflects a thought process and emotion. Very nice. The animator could have just as easily had her reach in and remove the blanket without the hesitation. This is more effective.

She sniffs the baby. This keeps Kala firmly in the ape world even though she is being humanized.

I'm not crazy about the diaper sniffing. Too much of a gag. The sequence was going just fine without that, and it didn't add anything to the mix.

Kala's facial expression turns to love as she cradles the baby, just before the tiger sequence begins. Notice how gentle she is.

Chapter 3: "A Narrow Escape"

The Sabor sequence is exciting and well acted. I like the way both Kala and the tiger strategize to defeat one another, and I like that Kala has more human-smarts than the tiger, a trait that is decisive in her victory.

Chapter 4: "Adopted"

We enter fully into the ape world and discover that the apes all talk like humans. This completes the process of humanizing them so that we in the audience can empathize and follow their story.

The male-dominant relationship between Kerchak and Kala is clearly defined. When Kerchak roars his disapproval of the human baby, it is crystal clear that he is calling all the shots.

Take a close frame-by-frame look at the moment after Kerchak roars ferociously and just before he asks Kala, "Was he alone?" You want to animate thoughts, yes? Notice how Kerchak glances to his right? He is weighing the reaction of the other apes against what he will gain by expelling the baby. He has conflict with himself for a brief moment. Lovely performance.

Chapter 5: "You'll Be in My Heart"

This chapter presents an opportunity to hear a sweet Phil Collins song. There are no scenes in this chapter. By that I mean there are no negotiations. We see a series of quiet bonding moments between Tarzan and his new family, establishing mood.

Chapter 6: "Young Tarzan"

This is a transitional chapter without much conflict. Tarzan has a small amount of conflict with his situation when he runs headlong into Kerchak, but there is not any real danger.

Chapter 7: "Pest Control"

Terk tells his buddies that he'll take care of things and send Tarzan back home. Notice the transition in his demeanor when he turns to Tarzan and starts schmoozing. This is another moment you can examine on a frame-by-frame basis to see how the animator captured Terk's individual thoughts.

There are a couple of clear negotiations in this chapter, first between Terk and his friends and then between Terk and Tarzan.

Chapter 8: "Baby Tantor"

Baby Tantor has a completely different rhythm and power center than the older elephants, and he is very humanized. Notice how he stamps his foot in the water like a human child when he gets exasperated?

The older elephants have a very low and heavy power center until young Tarzan gets one of them by the tail. At that moment, confidence (low power center) changes abruptly to fear and the power center shifts upward. That is when they all begin jumping around crazily in the water. Actually, this works the same way in humans. **When we are threatened, we get a huge adrenaline rush and our blood goes immediately to our extremities so we can fight or run away. This kind of automatic reaction was key to our survival in prehistoric times.**

Chapter 9: "Piranha"

Elephant stampede! This is a big action sequence that is worth studying slowly for all of its detail.

Notice that as the elephants stampede into the apes' nesting area, two apes are eating bark or twigs from trees. The elephants interrupt this activity. The acting lesson is that **your characters should always play an action until something happens to make**

them play a different action. The two apes could have simply been sitting and gazing at the sky, but that would not have been active enough. For the sake of discussion, consider this variation: If one of the apes was trying to dislodge a particularly difficult-to-reach branch or frond, then there would have been the element of conflict in the moment—and it would have been more theatrical. The elephants would still have interrupted things, though.

Chapter 10: "Outcast"

The character of Terk, voiced by Rosie O'Donnell, is unrelentingly over the top in my opinion. I suspect this is because there were a lot of video references of Rosie herself. A little bit of Rosie goes a very long way because she tends to be shrill and is not a very good listener. **Acting is reacting.**

The sequence between Kerchak and Kala is strong. There is a clear negotiation, and the conflict is between characters. From Kerchak's perspective, he wins if he gets rid of Tarzan; from Kala's perspective, she wins if she calms Kerchak down.

Tarzan is humiliated and the resulting emotion is sadness. Sadness leads to the action, which is for him to run away.

Chapter 11: "Hand to Hand"

There is an exquisite moment in this chapter. Tarzan places his hands against Kala's. That is when it hits him that, without any doubt, he is of a different kind than his "mother." The self-realization and shift in emotion in that moment is just wonderful acting. Look at it slowly and you will see each individual thought. Acting doesn't get much better than this.

Chapter 12: "Son of Man"

Tarzan grows up during a fast-moving and inspirational Phil Collins tune. He becomes a pretty good ape after all. Check out the skateboarding in the tree branches late in the chapter.

Chapter 13: "Monkeying Around"

After Tarzan unsuccessfully scares Kala, he sits on the tree limb in front of her. Note how he reaches for the fruit. He uses his foot.

Chapter 14: "Sabor Attacks"

Tarzan and Sabor fight to the death. I went through this action sequence several times slowly and every single move is motivated. Tarzan is continually thinking and strategizing. Sabor is a lower-intelligence animal and relies purely on instinct.

In terms of performance, however, the magic sequence is the one between Tarzan and Kerchak, in which Tarzan presents him with the dead cat. There is no dialogue at all, but there are several transactions going on, which is why it is good acting. Kerchak is so ashamed at the beginning of the sequence that I almost thought he was ready to abandon his position of leadership and slink away. Tarzan saw that, too, which is why he took the cat to him. Notice Tarzan's body language after he lays down the cat. He bends over in a position of complete subservience to Kerchak. The two of them exchange looks, and there is another transaction. If Kerchak accepts the offering, it might be construed to be unearned. His fate is now tied to Tarzan's. At the end of that negotiation, Tarzan has at last earned Kerchak's total respect. The rifle shot interrupts what could have turned maudlin if the animators had extended the moment. Excellent timing from an emotional perspective.

Chapter 15: "Explorers"

Note the way Tarzan finds and examines the spent bullet casing. He first smells the gunpowder and follows the scent. When he finds the casing, he does not immediately pick it up. He nudges it with his finger to see if it might move or something. It is only after he is satisfied that this is not a living

165

thing that he picks it up. This makes perfect sense if you think about it. The closest thing to a bullet Tarzan has ever seen is probably a rock. He certainly has never seen man-made metal. Our minds work in a sequential way, comparing what we see to other things we have seen in the past. It is impossible to understand the concept of "furniture" until you first understand "table" and "chair." A bullet casing fits nowhere in Tarzan's frame of reference. It will get a heading all its own. This sequence is very well observed.

There isn't a lot of acting going on in the rest of the chapter. Mainly, we are meeting Clayton, the Professor, and Jane. Note how high the Professor's power center is and how much he gesticulates. Clayton's power center is in that gun. He holds it low, about groin level, a lot.

Chapter 16: "The Baby Baboon"

Jane gets up close and personal with a baby baboon. The primary importance of this sequence is so that Tarzan can study their interaction from up in the trees. The scene is structured okay, but there isn't very much conflict. Jane plays actions as she studies the baboon, and the conflict is that the baboon won't cooperate.

Chapter 17: "Tarzan to the Rescue"

There are wonderful visual effects and action sequences in this chapter. Not a whole lot of acting, though, because there isn't much conflict. Jane looks like Mary Poppins to me, and Tarzan is the guy I want watching my house while I'm on vacation.

Chapter 18: "Treetop Introductions"

Study the getting-to-know-you sequence a couple of times slowly. The acting is marvelous and unhurried. Notice how the characters listen to one another. It can be difficult to animate a character who is listening and not speaking. That is because **listening should be active, not passive.** There is a mental searching going on when you are intently listening, a processing of the information. You are deciding upon and choosing responses. Notice also the shifts in emotion. Tarzan is almost childlike with his learning process. **We humans learn through a process of mimesis.** A young baby will stick her tongue out at you if you stick yours out at her. Hold your hand up to a baby's face, and she will probably put hers on yours. And, of course, we have the excellent moment when Tarzan puts his hand against Jane's. The nonverbal response after that is almost a Miyazaki moment. That is a long hold for Western animation. Tarzan's studying of Jane's body, including lifting her dress, is well observed. Her reaction to him maybe pushes the envelope just a bit. Her natural reaction would probably be more fear than delight given that she is totally vulnerable in this alien tree world, but I realize the storytellers need to get these two characters involved pretty quickly. For both characters, this is an adrenaline moment.

Chapter 19: "Trashin' the Camp"

This zany musical sequence was probably fun to animate but it doesn't add much information to the story. We get a look at how the safari travels, complete with a grandfather clock and a library of books.

You can look at the chapter beginning with Kerchak's entrance if you want to examine performance. The great ape sniffs Jane and recognizes the human smell. Kala enters and he exchanges a quick glance with her that says, in effect, "I told you we would have trouble with humans if we kept Tarzan. . . ." Without another look at Jane, Kerchak leads all of the other animals off into the forest. Tarzan has conflict with himself and with his situation. He does not understand why he is so attracted to Jane; he is also attracted to his ape family. He wavers between staying with Jane and going with Kerchak, Kala, and the others. The elephant makes the decision for him.

Chapter 20: "Jane's Rant"

This sequence doesn't have a lot of give-and-take, nor does it have a lot of theatrical structure. Jane is hyperexcited about her adventure and evidently not a bit frightened. The most significant acting moment is at the very end when she says the words, "Tarzan the ape man." Emotion tends to lead to action. Notice how the beginning of love softens and calms her.

Chapter 21: "Tarzan Confronts Kerchak"

Kerchak is unwavering in his transaction with Tarzan. There is not a chance that he will change his mind about avoiding the humans and therefore this is not a true negotiation. **Remember, in a negotiation, there must be a way you can win and a way you can lose.** Tarzan tries to change Kerchak's mind so, from his perspective, there is a negotiation. Note: yes, it is entirely possible for Tarzan to be having a negotiation while Kerchak is not. Each character plays his own actions, has his own objectives and obstacles. If these were live actors presenting the same scene in front of me, I would encourage Kerchak to maintain at least a remote possibility of capitulating to Tarzan. It would make the scene a bit more dynamic.

Jane, as it turns out, has great potential as an animator. She draws a really excellent likeness of Tarzan. The significant acting moment is when she completes drawing his eyes and once again swoons with love. Her father's reaction to the reality of love is sort of charming. It is the best acting moment so far for the old man.

Clayton, so far at least, has not displayed much depth or introspection. The only emotions I have seen him express are fear and happiness. **There are seven possible human emotions: surprise, disgust, anger, fear, happiness, sadness, and contempt.** (See my book *Acting for Animators* and also *Emotions Revealed,* by Paul Ekman, Times Books, 2003.)

Chapter 22: "Tarzan Drops In"

Tarzan examines Clayton. I like the moment when he literally climbs up him, trying to look in his mouth. Note also that, when he gets close to Jane, he smells her hair. Love is in the hair. (Sorry, I couldn't resist.)

The primary acting lesson is in the way that Tarzan processes new information. We can see how pleased he is with himself when he erroneously identifies the piece of chalk as a gorilla.

Chapter 23: "Strangers Like Me"

This is an expository chapter. Under another Phil Collins song, we see Tarzan learn about the outside world. There are not a lot of negotiations in the scenes, but there are some poses that reflect emotions. The feelings between Jane and Tarzan deepen.

At the end of the chapter, we have a new element to consider. Tarzan can now understand at least some English. This time, when Jane asks if he will take them to the gorillas, Tarzan is in conflict with his situation and with himself. Part of him wants to show off his gorilla family; the other part of him wants to protect them and to do Kerchak's bidding.

Chapter 24: "The Boat Arrives"

Jane has her best acting moment so far. Focus on her scene with Tarzan. Her objective is to get him to go to England. She has conflict with the situation, mainly, but the conflict shifts into conflict with another person as Tarzan better realizes what is being negotiated. His objective is to get her to stay, and he has consistent conflict with another character, namely Jane. If she stays, he wins, and if she leaves, he loses; from her perspective, if he goes, she wins, and if he stays, she loses. The magic element in this sequence is that both characters waver. Tarzan is actually considering what it means for him to go with her. Jane is actually considering what it means if she stays. She runs away in tears, unable to resolve the negotiation yet. Her running away keeps the tension in the scene high.

Clayton's objective is to get the gorillas, and his obstacle is that Tarzan has a wholly different value system. That explains why Clayton gives Tarzan the glass of whiskey. Push is coming to shove, and Clayton wants to lower Tarzan's resistance. He gives him whiskey (which Tarzan conspicuously does not drink) and tries using Jane's affection as a gambit. This negotiation resolves itself when Tarzan capitulates and agrees to take Jane to see the gorillas.

By the way, at the top of this chapter, Tarzan entered carrying a bouquet of flowers. That was nice. A character needs to have a reason for entering a scene. He came to give Jane flowers. **You play an action until something happens to make you play a different action.** When he arrived, he unexpectedly discovered that the camp was being struck. That is when his objective shifted to keeping Jane here.

Chapter 25: "Distracting Kerchak"

This is a simple low-level negotiation that serves mainly to get Kerchak out of the way momentarily.

Chapter 26: "Meeting Tarzan's Family"

When Tarzan says of Kala, "She's my mother," note that he touches his heart. That is a psychological gesture. (See *Lessons* *for the Actor* by Michael Chekhov.) A gesture is not necessarily an illustration of a spoken line. If he were illustrating the line, perhaps he would point at Kala, or maybe he would grab Jane by the arm to make certain she understands. Instead of that, he gently touches his heart. This is nuanced acting and is very powerful. If you understand how to use the psychological gesture, it will greatly empower your character animation.

I want to also point out Kala's reaction to the presence of humans. It is very apelike. When you look at Tarzan and then at Kala, you can see that he has now moved to the human side of the evolutionary equation. It is a subtle but poignant acting moment.

Chapter 27: "Tarzan Defies Kerchak"

Tarzan's objective is to save Jane and the others from Kerchak's attack, and he successfully wins that negotiation. But the price is dear, costing Kerchak his self-esteem as a leader. Suddenly, Tarzan feels isolated from his gorilla family. He is torn between two worlds. He has conflict with his situation. When he runs away at the end of the sequence, it has the same effect as when Jane ran away in Chapter 24. It keeps the tension high.

Notice that when Kala approaches Tarzan at the end of the chapter, she is once again more humanlike.

Chapter 28: "The Truth"

This chapter is an extended acting class. First of all, notice how the atmosphere in the old tree house affects the movement and behavior of both Tarzan and Kala. Second, notice how Tarzan is emotionally affected by the piece of cloth he picks up. **In acting, we call that a "sense memory." The smell of frying bacon, the feel of soft velvet, the feel of your mother's favorite necklace in the palm of your hand. . . . Each of these things stimulates an emotion.** Stage actors use this technique all the time.

The farewell scene between Tarzan and Kala is heartbreaking. Who among us would find it easy to say good-bye to a loving mother? Their final embrace brought tears to my eyes. **Acting has almost nothing to do with words.**

Chapter 29: "Clayton's Trap"

Tarzan learns a terrible lesson about humans. They have the capacity for cruel betrayal. The expression on Tarzan's face when he learns the truth about Clayton's motives is powerful. Given that this is animation, it is quite an artistic achievement to allow us to see a moment of true introspection.

Chapter 30: "We Got a Boat to Catch"

Tantor saves the day. Well, there are credibility issues by the boatload in this chapter, but never mind. The story needs to move along so that Tarzan can do his thing.

Chapter 31: "Ambush"

There is not much room for subtle acting in this chapter. Big ambush, big reactions, and a big rescue.

Chapter 32: "A Fight to the Finish"

Clayton's facial expression at the beginning of this chapter reminds me of Jack Nicholson in the movie *The Shining*, when he says, "Heeeere's Johnny!" The man is crazed and obsessed.

When Tarzan has the rifle at Clayton's throat, he must make a moral choice. This is proof positive that he is human. A moral choice is a very complex matter.

I like the symbolism of the sword piercing the ground after Clayton hangs himself. He who lives by the sword dies by the sword. Tarzan's "Oh, no" is interesting and maybe not totally credible. I can't see why Tarzan would regret the death of this man. It is a wee bit too noble for my taste. I wish he had simply looked at Clayton hanging there and then averted his eyes, perhaps in regret, but without saying "Oh, no."

Chapter 33: "My Son"

After Kerchak dies, Tarzan makes an almost imperceptible gesture. He gently chucks Kerchak under the chin. You will see animals do this kind of thing, but not humans. An animal will still try to rouse the dead, uncertain of the moment of death. A human knows right away what death means. I found that gesture to be extremely moving, even more than the shades of emotion Tarzan goes through as he realizes that he must now take Kerchak's place as the leader. **This is an adrenaline moment for Tarzan. He will never forget the day that Kerchak died.**

Chapter 34: "Good-byes"

Tarzan and Jane join hands again. Notice that Tarzan's hand is at first closed like an ape's. Then he purposely opens it to fit against her palm to palm. Once again, Glen Keane shows why he is one of the best. A powerful performance is made in such small details.

When the Professor urges Jane to stay, I wish he had not chuckled. Yes, this is a moment of joy, but it is also a moment of loss. This is why people cry at weddings. The Professor would be happy for Jane but sad for his own loss. He is an old man. He likely will never see her again. This kind of reaction would have better set up the Professor's subsequent decision to remain on the island with Tarzan and Jane. Maybe, this being a Disney movie and all, an executive decision was made not to cut too deep here at the very end of the movie. Just guessing.